# In Timberline's Embrace

# In Timberline's Embrace

What An Old Lodge Taught Me
about What's Worth Keeping

JEAN L. WAIGHT

RESOURCE *Publications* • Eugene, Oregon

IN TIMBERLINE'S EMBRACE
What An Old Lodge Taught Me about What's Worth Keeping

Copyright © 2025 Jean L. Waight. All rights reserved. Except for brief quotations in critical publications or reviews, no part of this book may be reproduced in any manner without prior written permission from the publisher. Write: Permissions, Wipf and Stock Publishers, 199 W. 8th Ave., Suite 3, Eugene, OR 97401.

Resource Publications
An Imprint of Wipf and Stock Publishers
199 W. 8th Ave., Suite 3
Eugene, OR 97401

www.wipfandstock.com

PAPERBACK ISBN: 979-8-3852-3484-4
HARDCOVER ISBN: 979-8-3852-3485-1
EBOOK ISBN: 979-8-3852-3486-8

VERSION NUMBER 121624

To Bill and Chris, who invited us to join them at Timberline Lodge, made it a rich, enduring annual tradition, and were there for these adventures.

Darting thoughts that give us a shiver of recognition, then
Disappear, a chimera in the mirror, the big one
That got away. We leave our trembling undone,
Little vulnerable fragments. We leave them as gifts,
Or curses, or messages in a bottle,
Genies in an unrubbed lamp,
For those who come after.

From the poem "Fragments,"
in *What If We All Bloomed? Poems of Nature, Love, and Aging*
by Victoria Doerper

# Contents

*Acknowledgments* | ix
*Introduction* | xi

1  1993 and The Slopes Were Ours | 1
2  Making Ourselves at Home | 7
3  More than a Playground | 14
4  Tossed Out | 18
5  Mountain Burglar | 22
6  Rooming with Rosemary | 27
7  We Get to Know the Staff | 31
8  A Winter Camp | 36
9  Off the Slopes and into the Barlow Room | 42
10 The Kids Are Growing Up | 50
11 Rainy Week | 51
12 We Rent the Blue Ox | 55
13 Losses and Gains—Timberline Goes Upscale | 58
14 The Wild West Buckaroo is Alive and Driving a Snowplow | 63
15 2014: Disaster in a Blizzard | 66

**16**  Cousins in Survival  |  85

**17**  2015: My Rescuer Tells the Rest of the Story  |  85

**18**  The Mural's Gift  |  92

*Also by this author*  |  97

*Interview*  |  99

# Acknowledgments

MY DEEP AFFECTION FOR Timberline Lodge would never have had the chance to sprout if not for friends Bill and Chris. It was at their invitation that my husband (also named Bill) and I made our first trip up Timberline Road, and it was their spark that created a not-to-be-missed annual tradition for a number of us snow-loving friends. I am in the best kind of debt to them.

Likewise, the Friends of Timberline, now approaching their 50th year, in concert with the long-standing Timberline management, prove the familiar words, "You've got to have friends." Together they are responsible for keeping intact the authenticity and spirit of this place. Through their quiet work, new generations can sense the love that was built into this lodge by the original makers of Timberline.

I am immensely grateful to my editor, Drue Robinson. A storyteller herself, she was fearless in stepping into the world of my story, and she helped make an episodic tale into a shapelier one. Her keen eye smoothed the prose, and she even lent her playwriting skills to a scene. In a word, her contribution was invaluable.

Much appreciation and thanks goes to early readers Julie Edwards and Steven Ihde. Later, Laura Velm's enthusiasm and input buoyed me through yet another "final draft."

And special thanks goes to Bill Waight, whose close reading helped with many particulars, as, sharing the adventures with me, only he could do.

Last, grateful acknowledgement is made to *Cirque: A Literary Journal for the North Pacific Rim* (Anchorage, AL) for providing a vibrant regional journal, in whose pages an earlier version of the present chapter 15 appeared under the title "Through the Floor," in 2015.

# Introduction

A FEW MILES FROM the Columbia River the Oregon mountain stands in a February dawn, its shape a thing of beauty—like Mt. Fuji but with a rugged Cascades mass and the jagged interest of a secondary peak high on a shoulder. Smaller rock outcroppings too sharp to hold a full mantle of snow give way to smooth white fields. The still slightly pinkish dawn does not reveal fissures, or even the presence of a blue crevasse, but they are there, too. The mountain is quiet, majestic, as though made for long, searching gazes.

The scene is without human scale until you spot a brown something halfway down the southern flank. This is clearly not an outcropping—not made by volcano or earth movement. Nearer now, a graceful stretched-open "L" reveals lines that are straight and human made. A handsome building, the heavy timbers are counterpointed by a steep pitched roof, which in turn yields to a small upsweep at the eaves, like an old-fashioned ski jump. The wings of the ell come together at a central structure that rises several stories higher and is crowned by a massive chimney and a 750-pound bronze weathervane.

Closer still, you see carved figureheads. Bear. Ram. They jut out at corners as finials where thick timbers extend from the interior. A sculpted snowdrift covers the first story and a half, leaving much of a huge antique picture window on the second floor to reveal to those within the lightening sky and the mountain's peak. The snowbank blocks the bottom of the window, and down at one dim corner, two eyes blink, looking in.

Timberline Lodge, Mount Hood. This is a place like no other. While you are absorbed in scale and detail, and charmed by both, another dimension may sneak up on you. The present intermingles with the past here in a singular way. I have found that if I am quiet, the lodge's history, thrumming so near the surface of the present day, delivers a kiss.

I'm an Oregonian by birth, perhaps influencing my view. But from my first visit to Timberline Lodge I sensed something special. And over a thirty-year span of February visits, it is not too strong to say that the soul of this place has marked me. I'm the third generation of my family to have come here in the decades since the lodge opened in 1937, so I do have family history here. Still, that doesn't begin to plumb what it means to love this old lodge, or what it means to have it become a part of me.

The events and impressions in this story vary from the comic to the mysterious and even to a freakish, frightening visit to life's very edge. I am sure the iconic lodge has imprinted itself on many sojourners in the years since its opening. I'm just as sure that the mountain itself must have left its imprint on all who who've trod its summers and winters through the millennia. What was long ago recedes and yet somehow remains with us. I still travel to this site where trees stop growing and the sentinels of snow, ice, and rock take over. Letting this place mark me, I also begin to ask what the places we love need from us. Even as they change.

1

# 1993 and The Slopes Were Ours

DRIVING UP THE SNOWY road, the temperature dropping as we climbed, we rounded a final bend and smack into our sight rose the lodge. Banked-in by snow and beautiful as an icon should be. Up close and somehow more than real. We get to stay here? My murmured question puffed in the chill and hung for a few seconds. Right off I knew this would be a great mountain playground for the forty-something barely passable skiers that Bill and I were. But there was more to this excitement coursing through me. Perhaps it was the astounding setting—the wild million-acre Mount Hood National Forest blanketing the land far into the distance, and here lapping up to the tree line. The clarity of the cold air, the ice-crusted conifers—wind bent, stunted, yet proud. Maybe it was everything: the magnificent weather-tested lodge, the compactness of having ski runs within mere steps, the glorious rugged peak rising behind the lodge. Even if I didn't know exactly why, at least for a moment I felt I'd been drawn here in a mysterious way. Like to a home I'd only dreamt of, or like a long-ago friend welcoming me.

What a lucky find. It was February 1993, and my husband Bill and I had been invited by our friends Bill C and Chris to join them and their young son Will at Timberline Lodge for a few days. My husband and I were still unsteady skiers, having taken up the sport around age 40. Bill and Chris assured us that Timberline had a lot of intermediate ski runs that would be good for us. And so, at our home near Seattle, Washington, we had packed up and headed to Oregon.

The sweet feeling I'd had at our arrival in the small parking lot was soon disrupted. When I stepped inside the lodge, first through the dark Quonset-style breezeway that protects the entrance during winter months, and then pushing open the heavy wooden doors, the acrid tang of an old oil burner assaulted my nose. I'm not a fan of smelly antiques—it wasn't love at first sniff. In fact, if we weren't arriving too late now to cancel our reservation, I might have suggested to Bill that we take the Timberline road back down to Government Camp, the mountain town on the highway, and look for a place to stay there. But, fortunately, the smell was only at the entry. And it happened to be right in front of a welcoming mosaic mural in yellows and blues. Over the years, upon arrival, we were always greeted by the same mosaic, nine feet tall and seven feet wide, a brown bear figure a bit primitively depicted, along with a leggy rhododendron, a deer, and ironically, a skunk, as if to say, Sure, there's an odor here; you can live with it. Indeed, over time the oil burner tang became familiar enough, reliable enough, to make me even feel affectionate about it.

Bill C, an expert skier, could ski anywhere, but chose this resort as a great destination for the family. While he enjoyed skiing the challenging runs, those labeled with the insignia of a black diamond, the resort also served up some easy trails, ideal for teaching little Will to ski. An abundance of intermediate trails allowed Chris relaxing days on the slopes. I wasn't a natural by any stretch, but Bill and I followed Chris.

Skiing starts right outside the lodge doors, a lovely human-scale compactness not found at all ski resorts. With only a few steps carrying one's skis across the parking lot, we could ski down "Pucci," named for the 1970s fashion designer who had visited and designed a signature scarf for Timberline Lodge. After a quick warm-up on the beginner grade "Bruno," we headed for Pucci, marked with a blue square on our map as suitable for intermediate-level skills. Skiing Pucci, Bill and I mostly stayed upright, with some windmilling of our arms to regain our tippy balance, and a few falls when windmilling failed us. Chris gallantly stopped many times to wait for us. And when part of the time we achieved smooth speed and reasonable turns, we grinned like kids, and so did she. Pucci had us eager to line up again at the bottom of the lift for another go.

The top of Pucci did have me standing and chewing a lip in fear of the first drop into narrow steepness. Narrow due to trees. Beautiful, but I found myself casting an eye at the wide open terrain above us, and above the tree line. Wouldn't that be more perfect for practicing and honing our skills? Less time burning our legs in the defensive snowplow position?

At lunch we rejoined Bill C and young Will. When told which intermediate run they'd been on, my eyebrows I'm sure flew up and I asked how, you know, was that even possible? As Bill C chuckled at me, he painted the picture: a small figure hanging onto his father's ski pole, which was placed horizontally in front of the boy, and papa bear Bill C holding the ski pole firmly in place and hovering over his cub. Making his back ache, but giving Will complete freedom and security. So that's how, it dawned on me, a skier can start at age four and become a skiing panther like Bill C.

The weather was lucky the next morning for testing out the broad expanse I'd been eyeing—clear and bright. So the three of us made our way across the slope past the top of the Pucci lift and over to the fast Magic Mile lift. There quad bench chairs awaited us and we could shoot up a thousand vertical feet into the open. Up on this lift the wind was stiffer and I was glad for my insulation in a new anorak shell and ski pants over woolly layers. On a clear day such as this, the Magic Mile grants riders the chance to twist around on the ride up for a grand view of Mount Jefferson to the south. Just like skiers of another time did when Timberline installed the first Magic Mile lift in 1939. I liked knowing about this generations-long string of skiers I was joining. To see from this vantage point was to be a kid again finding the prize in a box of Cracker Jack.

At the top, the fast chair slowed and we were unloaded (more on that awkward proposition in a bit) onto a small landing carved into the snow. We had the choice of three long ski runs. Although they were all marked intermediate blue, from the top they looked a bit scarier than they had from the bottom. Chris, how about you go first?

She started off. Bill and I looked at each other, both of us feeling challenged, but we were going to go, so it might as well be now. With butterflies in my stomach, I tipped from the small flat landing to the first drop and soon was whooshing straight downhill. To pull up, I concentrated on controlled turns into wide traversing glides to cut speed when it built up to scary, which was nearly always. My legs burned. When I stopped alongside Chris, she pretended she, too, found the long run an effort, though she was a solid skier. I kept an eye on Bill's forest green jacket and multi-colored wool hat to give him plenty of room—as inexperienced skiers we certainly didn't want to worry each other, or worse, risk a collision, as embarrassing as that would be in these wide open spaces.

At the bottom of this first run, we glided back to the chair lift to do the Mile again, of course. It was too scary to continue but too fun to stop now. Approaching the loading area, we found to our consternation that the lift had shut down. Has something gone wrong on this pretty day? The lift operators remained at their post, and there appeared to be nothing they were working to repair. Then upon seeing us, they grinned and waved us in, cranking the lift into operation again. As they loaded us and one spindly teenaged boy we hadn't seen before, they confirmed what we already guessed—they were only running the lift as needed. It felt like the most extreme sort of resort service I could imagine—a ski area operating just for us. I didn't want to be that special, but I soon got into the spirit of this privilege, knowing it couldn't last.

We got to the top and scooched awkwardly off our seat, the tell-tale sign of inexperienced skiers, our laughably intense body language showing our fear of spilling before we could hustle off to the side, or of getting whapped in the back by the chair that followed ours. We teetered to the landing spot where we could stand aside to make adjustments for the run, getting our big gloves threaded through the cold-stiffened loops on our pole handles and wondering whether we or the boy would be the first to set off. It's funny how quickly a person can feel crowded after enjoying having no people around.

The teenager started off. Bill started off. Waiting a few beats, I started off. About halfway down, after many turns, and with thighs stinging I stopped and stood looking downslope at my husband. As I watched, Bill's turns became increasingly matched by the teenager's, their paths forming a double helix, each loop well apart as they slalomed wide, then crossing at the narrow waist of the helix. They passed each other closely, and next time, closer. Helplessly I saw that the boy's control was poorer than Bill's—a lot poorer—until, and against all probability, the two lone skiers collided. Even in the moment the old joke came to mind: the driver reporting that the other car was "all over the road," saying, "I had to swerve several times before I hit him."

Bill was upended and came down on a hand trapped in the ski pole loop. And so, on this first trip to Timberline, we became acquainted with the Red Cross first aid station in Wy'East, the day lodge just below Timberline Lodge. Bill's thumb ligaments had ruptured. His injury had a nickname: gamekeeper's thumb, named for the repetitive injury caused in bygone days when a manor's gamekeeper broke the necks of small game birds, with thumb and index finger against the ground. The same injury now happens instantly in a skier's tumble where the skier falls on a hand holding a ski pole. Apparently Bill was not the first to do this. We hoped for better luck next year. Our first visit to Timberline Lodge was still a tantalizingly good trip despite going home splinted and bandaged.

We would be back.

2

# Making Ourselves at Home

IN FEBRUARY OF 1994 we were too tied-down to get back to Timberline, but the following year even graduate school couldn't keep me from our second trip to the lodge. I skipped classes to match trip dates with our friends. Two couples in our group each had a kid in school, and by happy chance, Portland's public schools were in session when Seattle-area schools were on winter break, promising we'd again find the slopes uncrowded on our mid-week dates. We were in clover, and skied our legs to jelly. More than that, we began to poke around in the nooks and crannies of this rich habitation of art, iron, and old wood. And we began to establish habits and routines that soon blurred one visit from another as we made this 1937 marvel our own.

One habit served as the opener to our Oregon vacation and made sure that when we got to the mountain our daily cares were left behind and were in a frame of mind to immediately soak up mountain life. We'd recently moved some eighty miles north of Seattle, which lengthened travel time to Timberline. I voted for adding a night in Portland to our tradition, as any born-in-Portland traveler would do. Bill, too, was happy to have part of a day to explore the city. I do love Portland, a city that grew to line the Willamette River on either side, with Ross Island in the middle, making for a city laced with bridges like a wacky corset.

While in Portland we have strolled downtown on foot, checked out the Pearl District, the tree-lined Nob Hill's eateries, and the newly re-blossomed area of Northeast 28th Avenue near Burnside. Always, whatever else we do, we spend a couple of hours in Powell's Books. Once I steered Bill to Mount Tabor Park, an old friend. I spent my first seven years in Portland, and my Aunt Peg would often take us to this park. Showing it to Bill jogged other memories of crosstown, pile-the-kids-in-the-car jaunts. I can still hear Aunt Peg, my mom, and Grandma Winnie at the kitchen table mapping the errands of the day: "It's across Division," "We'll go out Powell," "Take the Hawthorne Bridge—it's faster."

Still, as much as I treasure my native Portland, nothing compares to waking up inside Timberline Lodge—at 6,000 feet—looking out at a mountain wonderland. As soon as I'm awake enough to read my watch I look to see if I'll be in time for the lodge's tea and coffee service, which ends when the dining room opens at 7:30. Usually the answer is yes, there is still time. I head for the first floor into the common area around the fireplaces, my slippers silently padding over the satin smoothness of a white oak floor wavy with wear. At this early hour it is quiet, save for the soft creak of floorboards, or the crackling of a friendly fire. Other early risers are at the serving table getting their coffee, and they are also hushed, as if to keep the spell going, murmuring the barest of greetings or helping each other find the half-and-half. We gaze out the big picture window, then scatter to nestle on the davenports and broad-armed chairs around the center chimney column.

This stone chimney deserves its own description: it has six sides, housing three fireplaces on alternating faces of the hexagon. Each is inset with a timber lintel, the pale, unfinished wood a contrasting touch in the stone. Light and warmth spills from piles of crackling wood resting on iron fire dogs bracketed by giant, hand-wrought, impossibly graceful curled andirons.

It takes another vantage point to appreciate the full grandeur of this chimney column. Each time I walk up to the mezzanine level, I stop at the railing of the gallery walkway, whether or not I need to catch my altitude-challenged breath. I rest my forearms on the broad railing cap and survey the floor I've just come from. From this height, I see how the chimney serves as the centerpiece of this head house, as it is called, uniting the space even as it also divides it into more intimate sitting areas around each fireplace. A balance sensed, not shouted. Then I lean back and cast my eyes up this massive centerpiece to take in how it rises through the wide, airy opening, up, up, slimming as it goes until it is Maypoled by the radiating spray of beams supporting the conical roof. Those beams echo the arrangement of the davenports below—they extend like spokes from the hub of the center pillar. It's a wonderful unity of design. How to convey the character, the spirit of this rotunda? I think that the chimney's chiseled majesty, its sheer mass as it runs up through the center conveys a deep security that allows the common areas on the first floor and the mezzanine above it, to feel inviting, homey even. The head house is a big part of why Timberline Lodge in winter is like a gentle big brother—inside this lodge, you don't feel small; you feel embraced, safe. Safe, and snug.

After such a magical opener to the morning, breakfast becomes lively, and always with friends. Usually, we gather at a time we consider civilized, like 8:00. In the dining room, the buffet is scrumptious—eggs two ways, and oatmeal with roasted local hazel nuts, breakfast meats, an onion and potato fry, trays of cut fruit, specialty cheeses, and housemade pastries. For guests with a sweet tooth, there is well-syruped "timber toast." Once breakfast is done, we're on to the grunting, tugging process of getting into our ski gear and making an adventure of the day.

In these early stays at the lodge we naturally focused on downhill skiing, with bracing cold in our faces, followed by an uphill struggle, despite joyful camaraderie, to stay awake past 9:30. But wherever I am, a little quiet time always does me good, and one day I spent time at the ground floor exhibits. These exhibits, like a mini museum, introduce the lodge's history to casual day visitors. I strolled along a wall peering at a variety of small bits and pieces in cases. Then I came to a window and did a double-take. Looking in, I was surprised to see a re-created 1940s guest room. Preserved in the airless style of museums, what startled me was how close to identical this exhibit was to our room upstairs. I'd never seen a museum re-creation that looked the same as the guest room I was staying in. Of course, the guest belongings lying about wouldn't be mistaken for our modern versions—the woolen coat, lace-up leather boots, and other accessories of mountain wear dated the display room by sixty years. And in our room upstairs, Bill and I didn't have the hooked rug with the blue gentian in the center. But time, if not quite standing still for us, was at least nicely slowed down.

Initially, I didn't know what a blue gentian was. But the watercolor showed it to be a mountain wildflower. It dawned on me that the various watercolors of wildflowers in our room and the rooms of our friends were originals and dated to the 1937 opening of the lodge. A little faded, maybe, but precious in their artistry and botanical detail. Later, during an exploration on a summer trip, when the snowpack had receded to expose hiking trails, I discovered vibrant blue gentians blooming on the mountain meadows. Having seen commemorations in other places, including in the street names of otherwise interchangeable suburbs, of natural wonders after they were gone, I was entranced, and grateful, to find that Timberline's old watercolors are illustrations of what still blooms there. Seeing the actual flowers buoys my hopes that the fragile and fleeting can be lasting, if we let them.

The Friends of Timberline is an organization which, since its founding in 1975, serves alongside management in preservation efforts throughout the lodge. They make possible that sense of time almost standing still. The bright drapes are perhaps the first decoration that catches the eye in any room, and are a favorite of mine. With funds and workers from Portland's CETA program (Comprehensive Employment Training Act) the Friends have succeeded in making each new curtain they sew a faithful replica of the 1937 originals. The bold zigzag patterns are created from solid color cottons cut, pieced, and appliquéd onto a densely woven, bold yellow background—a triumph in primary colors.

One other exhibit in the mini-museum arrested my eye on that first perusal. It is a black and white poster of the emblems of a Native calendar—twelve moons. Taking in the spare beauty of each symbol, I naturally homed in on the emblem for the month we were in, February. It is called the "Hunger Moon." I stood before it and let it still me. I am freshly struck by my privilege as a warm and well-fed guest in this beautiful lodge. Struck by how easily people can run out of food in winter, how easily it could be me, or my ancestors, and what knowledge and work it takes, if one is outside of the world of supermarkets, to store food for winter. And how wildlife may have to tighten belts as well. This hunger moon symbol opened a spot of curiosity in me for learning more about winter on the mountain.

At the end of the day, with seasonal darkness having gathered around, we will tuck into a favorite alcove on the mezzanine gallery for card games with our friends. The actual bar, the Ram's Head, occupies the far end of the gallery circle. Wherever we sit, the bar and kitchen waitstaff always find us. With eight or sometimes upwards of 18 of us, this has become our living room. We get an upper body workout to match how the slopes worked our legs, as we move the bar's thick, heavy oak chairs and tables to suit the size of our party.

We have our favorite sitting area, but the entire mezzanine rewards a slow saunter. The oil paintings make the walls come alive with color and semi-abstract compositions. The many small nooks and crannies hold amusements, too. Black and white photographs from the 1940s and 1950s tell local stories. There is one of U.N. diplomat Adlai Stevenson with Pepi Gabl, who was head of Timberline's ski school back in 1956. Pepi's brother, Franz Gabl, the Olympic champion skier, gave me a copy of his adventure-filled autobiography when I met him by accident long after he'd retired. Small world.

One framed item is a reprint of an 1867 *Daily Oregonian* article chronicling two women who summited Mount Hood: a Miss Fanny Case and Miss May Robinson. Since this was long before the lodge was built, I wonder where they started from. They get points from me for managing heavy, long climbing skirts—these women were nothing if not proper. Photos in other alcoves document Hollywood's projects at Timberline Lodge, with stars such as Loretta Young and Clark Gable. Clearly, "The Shining" was not the first movie crew to discover Timberline.

Sometimes making ourselves at home in the Ram's Head is not by exploring around but instead simply getting off our feet. At times we need to plunk down on the butt-polished heavy oak chairs and refuse to move for a good long while. We had no choice after trying to ski in an unusual dump of powder snow in 1999. Powder isn't common in the Pacific Northwest, and it isn't easy to ski, so our first day on the mountain that February, Bill, Chris, and I took a "powder lesson" with an instructor named Autumn. Bill remembers Autumn trying to get us to do a jump turn, to which Chris, the best skier of the three of us, responded, "In powder? She wants me to jump? Not happening, it's just not happening." None of us were spring chickens. And unlike others of our group who, over the years, suffered pulled muscles, cracked ribs, and other mishaps, Chris was never going to do something foolish—although she was kind and sympathetic when others did. Minus jumping, we somehow got through the lesson with our young teacher and were quite happy when the mountain crew went to work patting down the fluffy powder, grooming the slopes for us.

So later, in our favorite mezzanine alcove, Chris dropped onto one of the heavy oak chairs and ordered up a Timberline Bloody Mary. While she tackled her drink's celery, tart marinated green beans, green olives, lime wedge, and liberal sprinkling of cracked black pepper, I went to work on a pint of Ice Axe Ale. That was payoff enough for me, but Bill felt I should be awarded a silk scarf, the same as those worn by Timberline's staff women. It's a deep blue that used to be called 'French Navy," or in a crayon box, "Midnight Blue"— the merest tinge of green making the blue sing. It is dotted with a scattering of small images of iconic Oregon sights: a covered bridge, a leaping salmon, a tall Douglas fir, a backpack, Multnomah Falls, a lighthouse, a seagull, Haystack Rock of Cannon Beach fame, Crater Lake, a pair of skis, a covered wagon, a tiny tent, and of course Timberline Lodge's beautiful face backed by Mount Hood. I wear this scarf often.

3

# More than a Playground

IT WAS AFTER I'D adopted Timberline as my home-away-from-home that I learned I was only the latest family member to come to this mountain. My father, Edward, skied Mount Hood in the late 1930s as a young man. It must have been a gas for the young Portlanders of the time, despite, as he told me, his first crude wooden skis being a challenge to stay up on.

Going back a generation, Dad's father and mother made a decision that resulted in, among other things, Dad's being a U.S. citizen rather than a Canadian. Isaac "Ike" was part of a German emigre family living in Alberta, Canada. Dad's mother, Ida, also German, arrived in Alberta as a minor in her teens, traveling with an older sister and emigrating without their parents—the family story goes that she was fleeing an arranged marriage. Ida took work with a doctor's family as a nanny in the farming community where Ike lived, and she and Ike married. In 1920, when Dad was just two, the family moved to Oregon. I can't be sure why they moved. Maybe the extended family didn't all get along; I know Dad didn't keep in touch with relatives in Alberta, though later as a family we often visited with his local uncle and aunt in Portland. Another possibility for why Ike and Ida moved may simply be that, since Ike was not a farmer like his cousins in Canada, he sought work elsewhere. Dad told me Ike was an excellent carpenter, who, for a time, built cabins in the Mount Hood vicinity.

Cabin-building may well be what initially drew Ike and Ida to Oregon. A historical society has documented over 80 cabins built by German immigrants Henry Steiner and his sons starting in the 1920s, a number of which are still standing (and grandfathered in places where no cabins are allowed to be built today). Each one-of-a-kind cabin was hand-crafted, and it may be that the German-speaking Steiner hired my German-speaking grandfather, or gave him a start. After cabin-building, my grandparents put down roots in the Portland area with their young family. Dad grew up on Ida's wonderful homemade potato bread and vegetables from her garden, as well as views of Mount Hood. I know her bread was memorably good because she was still baking it in the 1950s when, as a child, my sisters and I visited their home in Bandon, Oregon. I have an indelible memory of thick slices, with just the right amount of crust, topped with real butter, jewel-like honey from their own beehives and full-flavored home-grown blueberries, served to us with encouragement, in Grandma's German accent, to eat up.

It's remarkable how and why a family is drawn to a particular geographic location, and then by what alchemy a sense of place grows in the generations to follow. Timberline wasn't just a resort destination to me. Perhaps it was in my blood and bones for being a part of my personal history.

I have Mount Hood family history on both sides. My mother, Barbara, was a 19-year-old working in Portland when she set about climbing the 11,245-foot mountain. She and her sister Eileen climbed to the top in 1940, and Mom told of it with happiness and pride her whole long life. The ascent was scheduled for July 4th—the sisters and their fellas in a small party of six plus guide. They started from Timberline Lodge at midnight, a common method. Almost certainly they used the most popular route, walking up Palmer Glacier to Crater Rock, the large prominence at the head of the glacier. Mom told me they got to the top at seven in the morning. How magnificent the view must have been!

Climbing the mountain in summer was popular enough that the Mazamas Climbing Club organized trips, so this is likely how Mom's climb got set up. The Portland-based club was founded in 1894, two years after the start of the Sierra Club, with not only recreation in mind but with what we, today, call citizen science and conservation advocacy. The Mazamas Climbing Club lobbied Congress to prevent development in the Cascade Range Forest Reserve, and a bit later they lobbied to conserve the forest from sheep grazing. The club continues to this day. I was tickled to see that from the beginning women were welcomed as full members, and the Mazamas' website quotes founder William Steel as saying, "No climb is complete without them." This attitude seems to have been an Oregon trait—in 1912, a full eight years before women gained the vote nationally, Oregon adopted women's suffrage.

According to mountaineering sources, the usual climbing route goes east around Crater Rock and crosses Coalman Glacier on the Hogsback ridge, which takes climbers to the final approach. Then the ascent gets technical and a crevasse must be crossed. I wonder, given the 1930s popularity of this climb among inexperienced and non-technical climbers, if no big crevasse actually existed on the route at that time.

Later in life Mom added something to her story I hadn't heard before—that the climbing party had carved their initials on the wall of a wooden hut that sat, tied down by spike and cable against gale winds, at the summit.

There is no hut, wooden or any other construction, at the summit now. I had no reason to doubt Mom's recollection of a hut in that inhospitable spot, but in trying to corroborate her account, I talked with a few people familiar with the mountain and its history, and I found no one who believed there'd ever had been such a structure at the summit. After all, how would any structure built from hand-hauled materials withstand winter blizzards? Was Mom mis-remembering in her eighties? On the other hand, the peak, surrounded by forest, would have begged for a lookout structure so fire watchers might detect early smoke warnings.

The hut story remained mysterious for years. Then around 2013, the Mount Hood Cultural Center and Museum opened in Government Camp, and Mom's story proved correct. On the wall hung an archival black and white photo of a long-gone hut, looped over with strong cables and pinioned to the rock. The photo shows climbers' carvings, and the caption documents the hut's location—at the summit.

The incredulity of the others I had spoken with was understandable—the museum dug up a jaw-dropping 1932 Oregon Journal story of how a lookout hut atop the mountain got built in 1916. What determination the builders showed to get materials up there and work amid blizzards! The lookout was decommissioned in 1934, so it would not have seemed like vandalism in 1940 to carve up the walls.

Thanks to this museum, recorded details bring the past forward and enliven it for today's visitors. These stories prepare the mind to absorb the wordless feel of this place, the undertones. Countless footsteps, of indigenous people and newcomers, mingle here, inviting a certain kind of reverence.

# 4

# Tossed Out

ON A MOUNTAIN, THINGS are different, and a sense of humor comes in handy, along with a dollop of patience. The lodge staff set this very tone of good humor and patience—we seldom had more than inklings of the challenges they met daily. We just tried to do our part, working around the small snags we accept as part of the Timberline experience.

Unsurprisingly, the weather tops the list of mountain challenges. From our earliest visits, our group of friends dealt with any and all snow-related nuisances in good spirits. A heavy dumping of snow buried Chris and Bill C's car one year as it sat in the lodge guest parking lot, just 24 hours after we'd taken it to Government Camp and back. "Where'd the car disappear to?" was the question we scratched our heads about until the snowplow revealed it. Our own truck's door froze shut that year. Lesson learned: to our packing list we added a rubber mallet to break the ice seal all around the edges of each door.

A snag can be self-inflicted. Being perched on a mountain comes with another difference compared with vacationing near cities: if we forget something at home, we will probably have to work around what is missing. One early year, the same one with the car-burying snowfall, I forgot to bring underwear. Needless to say, I wasn't going to run down to Sandy or Portland for a store. So every night I washed my one pair and hung them up. They were mostly dry by morning. Well, damp-dry. I pack five pairs without fail now.

The Timberline Lodge of our early visits was a quirky combo of luxury resort and rustic camp. By rustic I mean not only the mountain cabin esthetic of heavy oak furniture and lampshades of scraped hide whip-stitched to a frame. When our group of a dozen friends would get together over meals or games, one or another of us always seemed to have a new small snag to report for our general amusement—something not working or a random creature comfort missing. And then someone would always say, "That's Timberline" to hearty laughter all around. Timberline was our oyster, and quirks were just part of the unique experience.

One quirk kept us uncertain of any robust connection between the telephone reservation system and the front desk. When we called in, the reservation desk noted our requested rooms—there were certain rooms that our friends requested, whether they were splurging on a fireplace room, or trying to pick a room away from nighttime snow-cat grooming operations—but, when we got there, sometimes the signals had snagged and others were enjoying our promised rooms. Glitches were resolved with apologies and fixes; I may be imagining this, but I seem to recall the management giving Bill and Chris a bottle of champagne for a mistake one year.

Bill and I suffered the weirdest error on our third trip. Our first morning, a Tuesday, we went skiing and came back in the early afternoon, stowing our skis and poles in the entryway locker assigned to our room. Tired and happy, ski boots in hand, we trudged on up on autopilot. However, upon unlocking our room, we were startled to find it empty.

Not just empty but made up as if awaiting new guests. Doubting our eyes, we looked up and down the hallway, and at our key and at the door and yes, this IS our room. So WHERE is our stuff? Our stuff, the stuff we'd left scattered from the little shelf in the bathroom, across desk and table and chairs, on the floor and maybe even in the closet, was gone, vanished. Our legs were rubber from skiing and we'd looked forward to a quick flop on the bed before finding some lunch. Instead, we marched down to reception. At the front desk, the scene went something like this:

"We're in room 214, and our clothes and things are gone."

"Oh, yes, it's all in the Bellman's closet. When you didn't check out by noon, we had to move your things out."

"But we are not scheduled to check out until Thursday."

"Oh." A pause. "We have that your reservation only extended to today."

"You thought we were here for just one day?"

"I'm sorry, we have another party coming in today for that room. Let me look here." Another pause while she pores over a record. "Yes, I'm really sorry for the inconvenience. We do have another room you can have."

"Well . . ."

"Room 215, across the hall. Here are your room keys," she said, handing over the brass keys with the room number stamped into them, and receiving our old room keys in return. "And here's the key to the bellman's closet."

We opened the bellman's closet. It looked like a New York apartment building's garbage pick-up was past due. Bunches of black plastic garbage bags nearly filled this roomy closet. Bill and I looked at each other quizzically—we weren't seeing our luggage, our duffle bags. The desk clerk said those plastic bags, those were our things. All our loose items, pretty much everything, had been gathered into garbage bags. We did not feel like laughing. Not until a little wine helped us tell the story to our friends at dinner. Eventually, as the years went by and the lodge got busier, Timberline implemented a better reservation system which worked—most of the time. Just as, with experience, I got a better packing system (lists work) and always brought plenty of underwear.

# 5

# Mountain Burglar

PRESIDENTS' DAY, FEBRUARY 15, 1999. After a late-afternoon check-in, we let ourselves into our room and looked out the smallish window to see Mount Hood's jagged white peak above us in the crisp, clear light of an achingly beautiful blue mountain sky. Bill remarked how lucky we were to be on the second floor—which put us well above the reach of the snowbank tucked up against Timberline Lodge, leaving us a view while darkening the rooms on the floors beneath ours.

The sun would soon be setting on this winter day. All was still. The trackless blanket of snow, dotted with ice-stiffened trees, whispered of deep, slumbering winter. I imagined any and all wildlife as inactive, soundly asleep. This winter mountain playground, this vista, was all ours. A thrill tickled my stomach, obscuring what I might otherwise have noticed—the merest tinge of loneliness when a place is left to humans alone. Maybe others felt it. Maybe that's why Heidi, the St. Bernard mascot, was swarmed whenever she visited the lobby with her handler—the lodge guests eager to get close, to pet her thick coat, to feel her panting puffs on their hands and faces.

My rumination quickly gave way to excited greetings as friends who'd arrived earlier emerged to welcome us. After swapping notes about the drive, we unpacked and joined together for drinks, and then supper, glad to be here, everything a familiar routine. But not routine for long. A message had come for us. Bill's nephew Christopher was making a spur-of-the-moment dash from Eastern Washington to join us, bringing his stepson Reise.

"They'll have their own room, right?" I said, intuition bothering me.

"I don't know." Bill shrugged. "We'll have to wait and see."

We had bragged up the lodge and the skiing to Christopher more than once, telling him our dates and inviting him to join us. It never seemed like it would happen with his busy work schedule. Had we ever gotten so far as to advise him to make a reservation?

We couldn't call now; this was 1999, before we all had cell phones, let alone transmitting towers that reached into wilderness. We scanned our compact, cozy Timberline room, its heavy round oak table, two chairs, a queen bed, small window, small bathroom, and all the old gold pine paneling I could ever wish for. More to the point in this moment: the minimal floor space. It was strewn with our big duffle bags, boots, and whatever else wouldn't fit in the tiny closet, half of which was inexplicably occupied by a standing fan.

Christopher and Reise arrived late that evening. No reservation. "Well, then," I said with unfelt bravado, "our room will work fine." We shoved some things aside, into the closet and under the table, and they unrolled their sleeping bags at the foot of our bed near the window. The four of us settled in for the night, the profound mountain quiet soon punctuated only by Bill's soft snoring and the sporadic clank of a pipe.

Nothing but silence from the guys on the floor. I, too, drifted off.

Not long afterward, something woke me. A rustling. A crackling kind of rustling. It seemed to be coming from the table, where we'd left a sawed-off cardboard box full of snack supplies. I thought young Reise must be up and hungry in the night. If so, why would I get this sense of a *struggle* going on? Now on alert, I raised myself up on an elbow and looked over at the table, straining to see. The heavy appliquéd curtain dimmed most of the moonlight reflecting in off the snowdrift, but the box nevertheless could be made out in silhouette. I saw a small movement. It wasn't Reise, unless his arm had miraculously become detached, boneless and undulating. No, what I was seeing was no human midnight snacker.

Could some creature have gotten in through the window we'd propped open? I tried to recall how far open we'd left it. A couple of inches, wasn't it? Three, maybe. Only enough to let out some of the stifling heat—Timberline's heating system had a mind of its own, and turning the wall thermostat down had no effect. In fact, it might as well have been disconnected for all the use it was—stuck on the wall just to give the guests something to play with. I shook my head, trying to make sense of what I was seeing. After all, weren't we up on the second floor? I guessed a squirrel could have gotten through if it could have climbed to the window from the snow bank several feet below.

But when my eyes could make out its form, I saw this was no squirrel. The dark body was longer than a squirrel's. This creature was slim, sleek and supple. The small hairs on my skin stood up in salute to an unfamiliar wildness. A squirrel is a wild creature, of course, yet not nearly so electrically wild as this creature before me. If there are different words for different kinds of snow, shouldn't there be different words for different orders of wildness? As my eyes focused in the dimness I watched this silhouetted apparition in her struggle to tug upwards on the unopened family-sized potato chip bag we'd brought up from Portland (at sea level) which was now, at 6,000 feet, blown up as if for a Macy's Thanksgiving parade.

The little midnight acrobat gave another try to steal our snack from over the rim of the stiff cardboard box, pulling on the narrow seam even though she saw me staring at her. A bold one, with small fierce teeth and claws, she gave me to understand that she was not particularly afraid of me. Yet those sharp teeth had nothing to bite into on the taut-flat surface so much bigger than her little jaws. Nor could her claws pierce the bag as yet, though clearly she knew there was food inside. She would crack it if she could just figure out how to get the blasted hulk out of that box. She showed no inclination to give up her struggle.

I had to do something. But what? In my nightgown I had no handy armor against sharp teeth. I would test the situation, one move at a time. I sat up. Not much reaction. I waved my arms. Her fierce little body jumped into a ready position facing me—holding her ground, agitated. With trepidation I picked up my pillow. She reared up briefly, then hunkered down, her stance shifting back and forth faster than I could see her move. She might as well have been levitating and coming down at a different compass point, like John Belushi in one of his ninja moves.

It was either wake the others and risk pandemonium, or take her on solo. I slid out of bed, my gaze fixed on her with what I hoped was a look of determination fierce enough to match hers. Perhaps she wasn't convinced the spindly figure she saw hugging a pillow was much of a threat; we locked eyes in a face-off. Seconds went by, as if in a freeze-frame. Then, desperate to break the impasse, I waved my pillow extravagantly, aiming to herd her toward the window. This finally broke her resolve. She jumped for the window sill and was out in a flash.

I hopped over one of the floor sleepers to get to the window, and saw that she had stopped on the snow bank. In the moonlight just about six feet from the window she turned her handsomely muscled body to face me again and give me a piece of her mind: "Yeek! Yeek! . . . *Yeek!*" Then in a blink she disappeared into her snow tunnel. I wasted no time ramming the window closed, even as my admiration rose for the svelte fierce wildness that was hiding, very much *not* sleeping, under the snow. The guys in the room with me slept on, undisturbed.

Morning came. The front desk clerk listened with strange nonchalance to my excited news of a weasel-like intruder. She smiled, said "We have just the thing for you." She turned into a back room, came out again, and handed me a wood-framed, heavy gauge "pine marten screen."

# 6

# Rooming with Rosemary

When February 2000 came around, Bill found he couldn't get away from work to make the trip to Timberline, so I invited my sister Rosemary and her eleven-year-old daughter Emily to go with me. Emily could try out her Christmas present, a new snowboard and gear, and I would get to show my Sis and Em around my favorite haunt. Leaving the guys behind working, the three of us drove to Mount Hood.

We knew Emily was new to snowboarding, so while I skied the first day Rosemary shepherded a lesson for Em. An athletically talented kid and cross-country runner, she was used to having her feet obediently planted under her, and discovered that sliding on a plank sideways was another situation altogether. This did not put her in an expansive humor, as I gathered later that afternoon. Still, when the gang got together at day's end, I noticed Chris and Bill's son Will with Emily, about the same age, hanging out together, if a bit shyly.

The others took Emily under their wing the second day on the slopes, which was a great gift to Rosemary and me. This meant I could spend the last two days of our short trip with my non-skier sister. With Emily in good hands, I ushered Rosemary across the scraped-bare pavement to explore the nearby day lodge, Wy'East.

For untold centuries, Mount Hood itself was called Wy'East by the Multnomah people. It was only after Captain George Vancouver's expedition in 1792 for the British Royal Navy that it became known as Mount Hood. Longboats left the ship waiting at the coast and traveled up the Columbia River a hundred miles. The magnificent mountain filling Lt. Broughton's eyes was a prize to be put on the European-made maps, and he bestowed on it the name Hood, after some forgotten British admiral who never even saw the mountain. Nevertheless, the name stuck, kicking aside the indigenous name Wy'East, as was the habit of a colonizing expedition. Mount Rainier, known to the Puyallup tribe as Tahoma, is another colonized renaming.

A step toward acknowledging the indigenous relationship with the mountain came when the Wy'East day lodge opened in 1982 a few hundred yards from Timberline Lodge. Adopting the name used by Multnomah tribes was a chance to begin changing the historical hubris that had named the mountain "Hood." Needless to say, I'm glad of this.

Wy'East opened just in time to ease the strain on the main lodge. The concrete stairs in the day lodge can take a pounding better than the wooden ones in the main lodge. With a cafeteria, a pub, a shop and equipment rentals, not to mention a huge parking lot just below the new building, Wy'East handles the daily comings and goings of a growing number of skiers up on the mountain.

Rosemary and I poked around the Wy'East mountain store and gift shop. We flipped through the bin of sepia toned photos from the early years of the lodge and other area history such as a print showing indigenous fishing before a dam was built. Another print was of dare devils skiing down the lodge roof, one of whom Bill C swears was his uncle. It seems I wasn't the only one in our party with family history here. The photo obviously recorded a year of tremendous snow accumulation.

I showed Rosemary all my favorite sights in the main lodge, both of us enjoying this tour. She especially admired Timberline's logo etched on tumblers in the smaller gift shop—the elegant, iconic snow goose, the same as the heavy weathervane on the rooftop.

In the end, Emily didn't stick with snow sports; she preferred non-slippery speed—soccer became her joy. Still, I'm grateful for the chance to introduce Rosemary and Emily to Timberline and to our friends.

In hindsight, the time I had with Rosemary at this beautiful spot became even more treasured. Rosemary and I were different personalities. A five-year age difference kept us somewhat apart in childhood, and our lives had further diverged in adulthood, as she moved across the country for many years. At Timberline, she and I talked about family, especially Mom, who spent weeks at a time in the spare bedroom she had built in Rosemary and Mike's home. Rosemary said wryly that Mom was a great sidekick but also a backseat driver, and not only in the car. We revisited old family times, including a reunion on the Oregon Coast several years after Mom and Dad's divorce. Our sister Julie had come from her home in Ohio, and the original five of us sat in the sand in the shelter of typical Oregon driftwood—a recumbent big tree with tangled roots, the wood gone smooth and silver—and shared a marijuana joint Rosemary had brought to see if our parents were game to try it. They were!

In these Timberline hours together, Sis and I rekindled our relationship. And just in time. Rosemary and I didn't know then, while enjoying Timberline, that within a few years cancer would cut her life short before her 51st birthday.

Mount Hood gave us a great opportunity to start knitting our sisterhood together more strongly, which buoyed me for the difficult times ahead.

7

# We Get to Know the Staff

WHILE IN PORTLAND we always preview the weather report for the Monday of Presidents' Day that we'll be traveling to the lodge. If lowland snow is predicted, we are prodded to an earlier start. Our route takes advantage of the newly built I-84 freeway that follows the Columbia River and bypasses a chunk of suburban development. After this, we drop south at Gresham to old Highway 26, where the countryside opens up and we pass many junctions for small Oregon bergs. We always have a laugh when we see the highway exit to Boring. A sign complete with a big tongue-in-cheek arrow. Maybe later, we say. Today, we'll let this highway take us to the mountain where whatever awaits us will be anything but boring.

As the highway begins to climb, if the weather is deteriorating, Bill and I exchange worried chatter the last few miles. Past the town of Sandy, how will the traction be? We drive through the small villages of Welches, Zig Zag, Wemme, and Rhododendron. Wide spots on the highway appear, telling one and all that snowfall is serious business—those are stop-and-chain-up spots. Years past, we've had to use a pullout more than once to grunt through a chain-up. This is a less frequent need on our trips now as February inches toward getting more springlike, but we're ready and have started using a better alternative, snow "socks."

The real ascent begins once we leave the highway at Government Camp for the mountain road ending at Timberline Lodge. Often this road is well plowed, or rough-ploughed and sanded, or melted to bare and wet—a walk in the park. But not always. One year well etched in our memories, the road up from Government Camp was more than dicey. It was snowed under, with a slippery layer that hadn't had a chance to bond to the older packed sub-strata. This was before we had our cold-weather Volvo wagon. We were driving Bill's small Toyota pickup, rear-wheel drive, with only two studded snow tires. At least, I think we had studded tires. We had weighted down the truck bed with bricks to give the studded tires a better bite into the snow and ice.

It wasn't enough. We felt the tires begin to slip and we pitched sideways a couple of inches. Bill's grip on the steering wheel was turning his knuckles white as he tried to find just the right pace and touch to keep us making forward progress. I offered an inopportune suggestion, to which Bill barked, "Not *now*, Jean!" That's how I knew just how taut he was. I grew tense as well. The final bend was coming up and I said "Almost there!" And then, at the turn, both of us clapped eyes on the bus that seemed to have instantly materialized in the road ahead. Even at our slow pace, we were gaining on it.

"Oh" escaped from me, and "Oh, crap!" from Bill.

Unfolding like a movie we knew without ever having seen it, the bus lurched and slid sideways and came to rest splayed across the road. Blocking both lanes. With more curses, Bill was forced to stop, maneuvering as far to the right as he could manage. The bus struggled with its fate, but it was stuck, and now, so were we. There was nothing to do but hike the rest of the way to the lodge.

We told the desk clerk we were here to check in, but that we needed a wee bit of help with our luggage. Actually, with our entire truck. The clerk was wonderfully accommodating—she took our truck keys and told us the parking lot guys would take care of everything. And they did. The parking lot guys (it seemed they were always guys) were great. As soon as the bus could be straightened out, they drove our truck to the lodge and called us so we could unload and settle in.

Another year, we got partway up the road and the truck stalled. Wouldn't re-start. Wouldn't even crank. We looked back through the cab rear window at our stuff, a big bulge tarped over and bungeed down. We hadn't packed light. What was underneath the tarp, we knew, were large ski bags, plus auxiliary duffles filled with swimsuits, flip flops, and thick terry robes—to ski was to want to soak afterwards in the hot pool—and thick sweaters, long underwear, extra boots, skis and poles, and all the other ski paraphernalia. That was only the half of it. Food and drink in boxes, a big cooler, and games for evenings—Pictionary, cribbage boards, Jenga blocks, Tripoley with beaucoup poker chips, even Mah-jong. Round out this pile with a snow shovel and bags of books we'd bought in Portland at Powell's.

So once again, we hiked up to the lodge. The front desk was again generous—Sure thing, the desk clerk said. We'll send a van down to your truck. Really? How perfectly wonderful, we said through our embarrassment. You don't have to bring in the bricks.

How to tip for such a service?

The truck did seem to have a ghost that had haunted Bill intermittently for the entire two or three years since he'd bought it from our brother-in-law Mike at the Toyota dealership. Now we had to have it towed all the way down to a shop in the town of Sandy. At that distance, an expensive tow. Worse, the mechanics couldn't find anything wrong with it. It started for them just fine. Stymied, Bill cast about for what to do. He recalled his original conversation with Mike, who apparently had felt bad to be selling Bill a truck with no extras—no extended cab, no gewgaws. Bill had asked what the basic truck came with, and it was like, um, a cup holder? So when he took delivery, Mike told him he'd thrown in a security device, an after-market thing he'd wired in. Now Bill, beyond frustrated at losing time on the slopes over this, and tired of the mysteriousness of the truck's problem, exclaimed to the mechanic, "Tear that device out. Just tear it completely out. I don't want it." And the truck never again gave us a moment's problem.

Another staff member we had occasion to meet was Timberline's handyman, or building superintendent. I wonder if his job description had included a requirement for patience. Here was a man who had an endless list of things that needed doing on the building and more popping up all the time. An older man, his experience with the even *older* workings of the lodge must have been vast. One time when I'd gone down to the basement level for the ice machine I saw him, through an open door, working on something. He let me poke my head into this hidden area, dark with a low ceiling, full of the guts of the 1937 building's operations, and possibly a dirt floor under it all.

Unfortunately, one year I added to his list of chores. Against my better judgment I had set my pearl stud earrings on the cup stand above the bathroom sink. I did this even knowing that the old brass cup stand fixture, while featuring a solid tray with a good lip to it, was loose and wobbly. I wouldn't set a glass there, but that's unaccountably where I set down my earrings. I didn't want to lose sight of them. Well, I knocked into this fixture somehow, sending the earrings up into the air. And as fast as my skinny arms and fast-twitch muscles are, my hands chased and couldn't get ahead of the earrings. Down they went. Did I mention there was no stopper, nor basket, in the sink? The front desk sent up Mr. Fix-It. He had to take off the trap—always a fun job—and pick through the gunk for my earrings. His name escapes me, but I'll always remember him with great appreciation.

Several bar and dining room staff members were there year after year and we got to know and appreciate them as well. Some of them had commutes that I wouldn't have wished on anyone, but they got there, through rain, sleet and drifting snow. Their constancy and familiarity added to the relaxed, home-away-from-home feel.

# 8

# A Winter Camp

It couldn't last like this. As more and more mountain-lovers discovered Timberline Lodge anew, and advertising ramped up, change came to Timberline, including prices that squeezed us. Bill and I, Peter and Mary, and sometimes other friends decamped to the less expensive "Chalet" rooms on the ground floor. The bunk rooms, as we call them, worked for us for several years. Never for Bill and Chris, however. They had their standards of comfort, and those standards included an en suite bathroom, non-negotiable. But *bunk* beds? Bill C and Chris threatened to come watch a demonstration of how I got down from the top bunk, but they never actually opened the swing doors to the hall of Chalet rooms, which soon became our hidden world.

The building being reliably buried in February to above that base camp level, what daylight we got in the bunk rooms came through the snow, or down window wells created by the warmth of the building. We immediately favored Room 8 and began to reserve it as early as October. The secret luxury of Room 8 was it was the only room to have one-story beds. Initially.

These small rooms did require resourcefulness. Wall pegs stood in for a closet. And no pegs over the little sink—Where to hang a wet swimsuit? The basement laundry, especially the dryer, seemed always busy, so when it came to wet swimsuits, towels, and the terry robes that got us between our room and the hot pool, we were on our own figuring it out. I tried bringing a clothesline, but there wasn't anything to suspend it from except the already loaded pegs, so the hangers we brought from home had to do, placed mostly on the pegs. Sometimes a newspaper or hand towel on the carpeted floor to catch drips. Yet overall, the rooms were comfortable and actually quieter than many of the upstairs guest rooms we had enjoyed. Down here in our Chalet *cave*, it was wonderfully quiet—we were less likely to hear snow cat operations, unburped steam pipes, or children's thundering hooves in the hallways.

Our room 8 idyll didn't last. Not too many years passed before we checked in to Room 8 and found they'd stacked the beds, and we needed to figure out how to climb up. We did like the gracious new space around the table and chairs, even if one or both of the cushioned chairs sagged in the middle, the springs shot. But the athletics involved in scrambling up to the top bunk from a short, saggy chair were daunting. Worse than getting up top was getting down. In the dark of night, sliding slowly down, on my belly or my back, and feeling with my foot for the waiting chair, made a trip down the hall something to dread. We asked the front desk for a ladder and never got one. Probably because these bunks didn't *come* with ladders. If management were to provide an after-market ladder there'd be a potential liability problem. We tried bringing a boat ladder made of treads on rope—but it wouldn't attach. And we tried a small stepladder from home—it was too short but helped a little. We had to face facts—the bed frame designer envisioned kids taking the top bunks by climbing up the slat structure at the foot of the beds. Oh, yes, we tried that, too, barking our adult shins and inflicting pain on our aging feet due to the narrow slats.

The housekeepers typically were skinny young snowboarders financing their mountain habit via this job. If I could catch them, they would graciously detach the top bunk in room 8 for us, without our having to convince the front desk, who I think frowned on minor alterations of guests' furniture. This was one of the reasons we prized room 8—it had the rare width to permit two beds against the walls. There are only a few bunk rooms for two. I don't count room 5, which is a claustrophobia-inducing closet. Yes, we got to know all the rooms. Friends Mark and Caren once took one of the ten-bed rooms for their big family, and Peter and Mary took a four-bunker the year that Aya, their former exchange student, joined us from Japan.

All these bunk rooms made campers of us, and the bathrobed trips in the night to the toilets are part of that ethos. Sometimes a previous guest would leave some sort of toiletry mess in the sink, or water on the floor from the shower, or would leave the toilet paper holder empty. Just part of camp mode; so pull out another roll from the bin, install it, and carry on. When I found out that these rooms had once been staff rooms, staying in their wake made me feel closer to the original life of the lodge. Aided by their can-do spirit, still somehow hanging in the air, we soon bonded with our cave.

On a typical morning. I will poke my head out to see if Peter and Mary's door is cracked open, the signal they are up. Bill has gone to wait with others for the dining room breakfast buffet, and I cross the hall to sit with Mary and Peter instead. Such world travelers, these friends are adept at making an amiable home wherever they find themselves, and gracious living follows them everywhere. They convert their small double hung window, about two feet wide, into a glass-front ice box by scooping out buckets of snow, which they drop into their sink to melt while they pat down a snow shelf for a carton of milk and sandwich makings. Mary is cheerful and happy even before tea and welcomes my morning invasion. Peter moves about in a tee shirt and sarong, pouring boiling water from their electric kettle into their Brown Betty teapot for a proper steeping. They take their tea in the English style, with milk, as Bill and I do. Peter is English; Bill and I are copycats.

One year I copied another practice of Peter and Mary's. I brought a pork roast I'd cooked the day before the trip, and bread, so we could be set for lunches. I had to get into Bill's first aid pack for Band-Aids after cutting my hand wrestling the slippery roast on a too-small cutting board. We soon abandoned our sandwiches for the French fries at the day lodge with Bill C and Chris. Other temptations to eat "out" included the bean chili that was hugely popular despite what the altitude did to the gut. Of course, some of those eating chili in the day lodge were on the mountain only for the day and would be trundling back to sea level before the gastronomic rumblings began. But we lodge guests ate it, too, and then headed to the outdoor hot pool, where the jet bubbles made the consequences not matter.

There is nothing like the Timberline hot pool for making new friends. After lunch Bill and I pushed through the door weighted with drifted snow and stepped down into the frothing water. There we found folks from the Greater Kansas City Ski Club. Did I hear that right? Missouri? They may not have mountains, but they do have enthusiasm for travel to western ski resorts. With snow falling on our heads we soon looked like a big brood of children lathered in suds.

I make it sound like we never ventured out from the lodge environs when it snowed, but we did. The Mt. Hood Brewing Co. often beckoned us to come on down to

Government Camp for a pizza night. I recall there were times not going might have been the better part of valor. Once, it snowed seven inches from the time we'd parked up at the lodge, and the cars were pretty well choked in. But, we were hankering for pizza, so Bill and I volunteered to take four of the group down in our Volvo wagon. Bill tapped the doors all around with his rubber mallet to crack the ice seal and raised the back seat into place while Peter set about shoveling. Even though his gloveless hands stuck to our metal snow shovel, Peter moved enough banked snow that, with Bill in the Volvo driver's seat and the rest of us pushing, then letting the car rock backwards, and pushing again, we got the Volvo out. We were younger then and the huffing and puffing out in the cold made that local "Ice Axe" ale and loaded pizza taste fantastic.

Certainly, Timberline Lodge allows our friends from three Washington counties a gathering place in a beautiful setting and away from our everyday routines. It is telling that Peter and Mary, the adventurous world travelers who rarely go anywhere twice, have returned to Timberline again and again. Bill C and Chris seem never to miss a year, even when we do—except, of course, for the two years of the pandemic. Bill and I simply fell in love with Timberline, as our friends seem to have, and get there as often as we can.

For me, this affection would paradoxically only deepen after I quit skiing. My appreciation of the lodge's beautiful, hand hewn, solid feel grew every time I viewed the video, "The Makers of Timberline." It is shown in a tiny viewing room tucked behind the ground floor fireplace. To see just how much the paying work meant to the builders and decorators in the midst of the Great Depression, and to hear in archival interviews how grateful they were for their short-lived jobs—Timberline went up in just eighteen months—always moves me. In the video, one 1936 story is emblematic, about the watercolorist who had painted in Europe in better times. The lodge decorators somehow located him in Portland and commissioned him to paint wildflowers for Timberline's many guest rooms. They found him in heart-wrenching circumstances, existing in a piano crate. I always have to pause at that point in the documentary and dab my eyes.

That isn't all. There is footage of men keeping a hand on a guide rope between one spot and another while working on the lodge's exterior in a blizzard, lest they be lost in a whiteout. I always hold my breath at the part where the undersized crane yanks loose one boulder at a time from a pile, the boulder dangerously bouncing and swinging before being coaxed into place for the foundation. A foundation that grew wheelbarrow by wheelbarrow of mortar cement, similarly lifted or *pushed* upward on planks, and poured on. The stamina of thin men who had quickly hewn tall supports from straight old-growth Douglas fir logs brought in from southwest Washington. For the interior, footage of the blacksmith artist creating the impossibly heavy andirons, working from a wheelchair, drawing the red-hot iron from the forge and bending it to form the graceful curl at each end—this astounds me. As do the seamstresses cutting, weaving and stitching from dawn to nightfall in a school house miles away. These were all acts of love infusing the materials and the fine art they left us. Marjorie Hoffman Smith was responsible for the unified beauty of the lodge interior and also designed Timberline's flying snow goose logo, saying she took her inspiration from the art of the local Tenino people. It's beautiful, elemental, and timeless.

# 9

## Off the Slopes and into the Barlow Room

I GOT BETTER AT skiing for awhile, then started getting hurt, mostly at other ski areas in the region, but one time was at Timberline when I was feeling overly confident and tried a small jump off a hillock. I lost balance and slowly sank backwards into a sitting position on the back of my skis. Skiers reading this will know sitting back is impossible in those boots. So I didn't have the normal luck of falling and having a binding release for me, and instead I ended up far overstretching a knee. I still wonder whether my yoga practice was a detriment that day—by contrast, a friend had a fall in the Mount Baker ski area, trying to protect a novice child skier with whom she was colliding. She did a clean job of snapping a knee ligament so that it had to be surgically repaired, but her knee fared better than mine over the long run. My knee did eventually heal well enough, only to have arthritis in my shoulders begin to announce itself; a sudden move with my ski poles and I would yelp with pain.

The day came when I quit skiing. It was probably in 2004. At first, I mourned the loss of the exhilaration of whooshing downhill, but I knew in my bones it was no longer worth the risk of damage.

What then? Bill probably could have skied with another family of our group if I stayed home. But I *did* still want to come to the lodge, be with my friends, see Bill's face shine with pleasure when he came in from a good morning on the slopes, of course eat good food—and soak up the ambiance. So, the next question became: If I were to keep coming here with everyone, how would I'd occupy myself while others skied?

My first thought was to bring books. I well knew that after the morning flurry around the front desk for lift tickets, and around the big fireplace as skiers locked down their boots—once all that hubbub cleared away a little after 9:00, the lodge went quiet. It was going to be simple to choose a quiet easy chair up in the main lounge. I could also bring my yoga mat for just the right out-of-the-way spot. The first morning at the lodge that particular year I happened to notice that no one, not a soul, was in the Barlow Room. My chest tingled. The thought of reading went poof. What was the sense in letting reading carry me away to other climes and places when I was overlord of a fantastic clime and place right here? I found I didn't really want to cast my mind elsewhere. Though I love to tap into what good writers have to say, I was already in a place that has something to say. I would listen. Look, and listen.

After walking through the lodge entrance, which is arched over by a corrugated Quonset hut-type roof covered in snow, the first thing front and center that fills the eye is the massive stone base of the fireplace column. Around back of it are the historical exhibits mentioned in a previous chapter, the tableau exhibits preserving a slice of 1940 in amber. To the right of the fireplace chimney a wide doorway beckons, flanked by cheerful hand-pieced drapes, drawn back to reveal, like a frame, the few steps down into a sunken room. This is the Barlow.

The name, Barlow, is storied in our American history; famous in the context of the wagon trains that came west in the 1800s. In 1845 many would-be settlers, including a Mr. Joel Palmer, acting as guide to his wagon train, had stalled near Mount Hood on the Columbia River, unwilling to try the dangerous Cascade Rapids. A land route was needed through the Cascade Mountains, a daunting prospect, but the pull of their destination was irresistible—the large, lush Willamette Valley that stretches southward from present-day Portland. Sam Barlow, heading another of the wagon trains, was already scouting a southern route through the Cascades when Palmer heard about the quest. Palmer found Barlow and joined up with him. But how could they plot a route when they couldn't step back and see through the thick forest? The only view good for surveying required climbing Mount Hood. Palmer made the climb to a viewpoint on the upper slopes. Now the Palmer glacier is named for him.

Barlow did build his road. His petition to the provisional legislature was granted, and he received a charter to construct the Barlow Trail—a concession toll road through this corridor. However, the best they could do was a rough job, and I wonder how many wagons, loaded with provisions and tools, rattled themselves apart. At one mountain pass, wagons had to be lowered on ropes down a 60% grade; this became known as Barlow Pass. Even so, Barlow's road was good enough to allow the wagons to make it to the Willamette Valley, a land of milk and honey in pioneer dreams. They gathered in the valley, having met up with the rest of their party who had taken a boat ride down the Columbia minus the goods being overlanded, and they all lodged in Oregon City, newly laid out in 1842, for the winter of 1845.

So, the Barlow Room gives a nod to the stubborn spirit of these wagon train hopefuls. I used to think of the wagon train era as belonging to the distant past, but as I've gotten older, and even more time has passed, my perspective has changed. The 1840s of covered wagons was only about 75 years before my paternal grandparents emigrated from a small rural town in Alberta to western Oregon, and it was only another 75 years before I started coming here to this mountain near the Barlow Trail. In lifetimes, not long at all.

In the context of the lodge, which was built mainly as a resort for various outdoor sports, the Barlow's early purpose was to house a raucous grill serving lunch to young skiers—including, no doubt, my father, in the late 1930s when the lodge was first constructed. In this *new* century, the Barlow is a game room. A nice, heavy shuffleboard console hugs the left wall; a ping pong table is also well-used, especially by kids, and an untuned piano sits on the right wall. In the middle are rows of seats for the nightly movie screenings for lodge guests, often "The Shining." Though the interiors in the thriller about a fictional Overlook Hotel were filmed elsewhere, "The Shining" made spooky use of exterior shots of Timberline Lodge in several scenes.

But for me, on a quiet, overcast morning, its contemporary purpose slid away and the past came out to play, a friendly past, nothing like the pull of Stephen King's malevolent ghosts and elevators full of blood. This friendly past was also nothing like exhibits through glass. In a funny way the past in the Barlow Room is alive, almost vibrating, touchable. I took my yoga mat down the few steps into the spacious room and unfolded it in the far corner. Above me I noticed a heavy, carved light fixture the size of a small canoe that graced the even heavier ceiling beam it hung from. The only window to the outside added a white-gray, bracingly natural light, and I began a stretching routine, somewhat sheltered by an immense supporting column, letting the muffled ambient sounds of busyness on the other side of the wall wash over me, keeping me connected to the resort of the present while breathing the thick air of the lodge's history. I felt serenely alive. I took many breaks from yoga to wander from one mural to the next.

The murals. The invitation issued by the unoccupied Barlow came not only from the quiet solidity of a foundation snug against the mountain, or of adze-marked pillars big enough to hide behind, or the expansive room's cracked beams speaking of decades. The still vibrant past is more in the band of murals that circles the room at eye level. Depicting outdoor activities in all seasons, the murals are individual scenes strung together. At first, they look to be worked in pale wood, painted thinly in oil paint washes, from intense to translucent. But peering closely, I could see that the substrate is not wood but linoleum, and incised no more than a quarter-inch deep.

In artist Douglas Lynch's hands, that minimal depth is enough to make the scenes pop forth with a sculptural quality. Moreover, the cut lines are impossibly graceful. Simple. Playful. Nothing stiff or static. I was in awe. It is one thing for an artist to stand over a sheet of linoleum and, sweeping freely from the shoulder, draw lilting curves with a pencil. It's another thing altogether to retain the freedom of those pencil lines while chiseling through linoleum.

The next thing I noticed were the colors. They are varied and often vibrant, yet all from the same gentle palette of 1930s colors that blend with the blond tones of the base material. In one panel, a grandmother cooks over a campfire. In others, hoe-down dancers bounce, tobogganers sway, a girl and large pack horse lean apart stretching the lead in a test of wills.

The mural depicting family camping in the forest made me smile. The foregrounded grandmother tends her cook pot, crouching on her stout haunches, while the rest of her family is arrayed about, all with concerns of their own. The scene brought to mind my own experience of family camping, and one particular trip that made me laugh out loud, right there in the Barlow by myself. It was a camping trip from my young childhood—it could be called the "Lake Incident."

*Scene: A state park somewhere in western Oregon, designed for 1950s car camping, with tent space, grate-topped fire pit, picnic table, and paths through the tall trees to the outhouses. It is summertime.*

*The all-gal cast: Grandma Winnie, Aunt Peg, a family friend, Mom and me (around the age of four).*

*After setting up camp and enjoying a picnic supper, it starts to rain. Looks like real rain, not just a passing shower. As the neighboring camp starts to break camp to leave, Mom remarks that the men at home are probably laughing at us now and expecting we'll pack up and return, damp and defeated. The others say "No way!" or whatever expression is current in about 1954, and tie clotheslines to trees, hastily rigging a tarp over the top. Thus tented, the picnic table makes a dryish room for card-playing by lantern light. Satisfied, Mom puts me to bed in the tent and the adults lean over their coffee (no doubt perked to the point that no one would touch it nowadays) and continue playing cards (probably pinochle), no doubt snickering about having the last laugh.*

*Meanwhile, my sleeping bag is getting wet.*

~ Mom, I'm in a lake.

~ *(From the picnic table)* No, honey, you are not in a lake. You just had a dream. Go back to sleep.

~ *(A little while later)* Mom, I'm in a lake.

~ We're all a little damp, Jeanie, just go to sleep now.

*Another little while passes. I'm getting wetter, and it's from underneath the sleeping bag. The air mattress is threatening to become unmoored from the tent floor.*

~ Mom, I really am in a lake.

~ *(Checking on me at last to discover a puddle of such dimensions it becomes clear we aren't going to sleep in the tent that night)* Well, I'll be!

I remember being toweled off and wrapped into my jacket during a flurry of camp-breaking activity, flashlights flaring as the adults scattered and consulted with each other in the dark. Then in my next recollection we are all huddled together inside the chosen shelter: a huge hollowed-out tree. I must have fallen asleep. Whoever was at the back of our tree tent surely didn't catch a wink because she got "huddled" all the way out the other side, leaving her backside in the rain all night.

The posted brief about Lynch includes a poignant, intimate story. He quietly put himself in the mural that's halfway through the series, the panel that depicts a happy evening of summer dancing. He's the standing figure watching as a glowing young woman shifts her affections to dance with a new beau. The dancing woman is Lynch's wife, and this mural secretly depicts his heartbreak. I wondered if there were other stories Lynch infused in each of the mural panels. It hardly matters now. All these decades later, I've created my own stories; the murals take my own meanings from my own past.

One panel in my chosen yoga corner that day—adjacent to where the first lunch counter had been—is nearly all off-white, blank, especially if seen from across the room. Repeated scrubbings, for no doubt the skiers lunch grill was a greasy one, must have rubbed away most of the color. The linoleum, of only this one panel, is deeply cracked.

Curious, I stepped closer. I could make out the image of a sweet young woman out for a walk in the woods. "Spring Walk" is the title. Her sweater, almost cream white now, shows vestiges of the burnt orange it once was. I could see that her plaid skirt was once green, since a corner of it escaped the heaviest scrubbing. Her skirt is actually a kilt, the front panel wrapping to one side and edged with short fuzzy yarn fringe down to the hem, which kicks up jauntily with the lift of her knee. To the right of her soft-booted feet, a pair of fat salamanders crawl, or perhaps swim in a faint stream. Her dog has a ruff that's collie-like, longer and fuller than the rest of its coat, and the long ruff is echoed in the fluffy spray of his hock hairs. He bounds ahead, turning back to look at her as if to urge, "Let's go this way."

Anyone would call this panel a ruin. Did the staff, or the Friends of Timberline, decide to keep it for its history? I took to it and was glad it was still there with the other scenes. And this particular Barlow mural panel was not yet finished with me. It would take a few more years before I knew why.

10

# The Kids Are Growing Up

In and around 2010, our group of friends swelled to eighteen. The small boy Will was now in college, and he turned his annual Timberline trip into a reunion with two high school friends. Their young energy was a kick to see.

I watched his brawny friend clamber up and hang from a huge beam between the fireplace and the Barlow Room steps, his hands reaching edges, his ankles crossed around it.

"Did your friend do gymnastics in school?" I asked Will. The sight tickled my reverent attitude toward those beams. No harm. Timberline was built as a playground after all.

"Wrestling," Will replied.

11

# Rainy Week

ON OUR FEBRUARY 2012 trip, every single day of the week it rained. Rain like a monsoon. Rain like it seemed it would rain for the rest of the year. Ironically, this was the year Bill finally took advantage of the annual lift ticket bargain that gas stations had been offering for several years.

Weeks before the trip, Bill bought three of these discounted lift tickets, only to have the mountain weather laugh at him. It rained sideways. This is not what ski goggles are for. His tickets were a waste. We were all at loose ends, but Bill decided disappointment had to happen sometime, and so he set a Zen tone for the day. It would be "Okay . . . that's all right."

We would need that perspective, because the next hurdle was that I couldn't get warm water for a shower in the communal ground floor bathroom. Seemed the problem was only in the Chalet bathrooms. Okay, *that* shower was bracing! Then, though I'm usually not one to spend any real time at Timberline in front of a computer screen, but with little else to do, I fiddled with this and that trying to get my email to send, and eventually discovered that the signal was out. Okey-dokey, that is futile, but I can resort to a book. The rain continued.

And . . . still, the rain continued. The parking lot was a river of slush. It was too windy to use the pool. Still, okay to all that. Time for a bit of yoga—really, just exercises the doctor had given me for my back. I got a sliver holding on to the pillar. *Oookay*. Went back to our room for my tweezers to pull it out and ran into would-be skiers Mary and Chris. They had actually gone out in ski gear and come back immediately. It was clear to all of us that here was a day for "Plan B" activities. So the three of us tried a walk on Timberline's recently constructed snowshoe trail. Maybe we thought the weather showed signs of letting up, or maybe we hoped once we got around the first turn we'd be out of the wind. I don't recall our thinking, except that we had come to Timberline for mountain activity and we were going to try anything. It was a blustery, wet walk—snowshoes not really needed on the wet, firmly packed trail. Our walk was sort of okay, but I was still hoping for something to go right that day. Hoping to find a highlight among the low lights.

"This has been a different kind of day," Bill said with a sardonic smile. Yes, it had been. But after waiting long enough, a highlight did indeed arrive. In the evening, several of us hoisted an effort to assist Bill, who wanted to try to get a professional-quality shot of the Charles Heaney painting, "The Mountain." This large oil, which graces the dining room entrance, shows its glory despite light that doesn't do it justice. A fusion of abstract, realistic and analytic sensibilities, the mass of "The Mountain" breaks down into facets. That would be artful enough as far as design is concerned. The genius, however, is in the dominance of vibrant colors and how they converse with each other. Charles Heaney's use of teal blue slays me each time I look at it. Not bad for a former sewer digger, he being yet another artist plucked from obscurity during the Great Depression. "The Mountain" is a masterpiece, a monumental work, inspired by Cezanne and the work of Heaney's friend in Portland, C. S. Price. It was completed in September of 1937, just in time for Timberline's dedication.

During our many visits to the lodge, we'd hunted in the gift shop for a professionally made image of this fantastic painting to take home. No luck. Perhaps because the painting hung in less than adequate light for photography, a professional shot had never been taken.

After Bill obtained permission by swearing to the lodge manager that he didn't have commercial intent, which was true, James, Peter, and I helped him set up his photographers' lights. (Yes, we tended to pack heavy.) We waited until after the dinner traffic had retired for the evening and then set to work.

I was thrilled to see the painting's colors under the bright specialty lights—not a yellowy "soft white" among them. I also got a kick out of experiencing a taste of what a pro photography shoot is like. Bill hadn't shot professionally since working for Seattle Opera more than thirty years ago, and this rainy-day activity was as close as I might ever get to being on a photographer's crew. We pushed heavy chairs into place as directed by Bill so the tripod, tall as it was, could be set atop them in order to get his large format camera higher still, then we turned off the lodge's area lights. James and I held Bill's lamps while Bill tested the lighting using a grey card, and finally he took six exposures. Of course, shooting film, we couldn't know how well any of the proofs would turn out. How funny to be using bygone technology to capture an antique painting in an old building. Even so, it was enjoyable and we went to bed hopeful.

How did Bill's exposures turn out? We got *close* to eliminating all the shiny spots. Not the perfection we sought. But the rainy day? In the end it turned out very okay.

## 12

# We Rent the Blue Ox

THE BLUE OX BAR is a tiny bar, an afterthought in the planning of the lodge. I guess the makers of Timberline were on such a natural creative high, not to mention working into the evening hours, that they gave no thought to a watering hole. When it dawned on the interior designer that the entire lodge had no bar, a little room intended for firewood storage was commandeered, and the small, windowless Blue Ox was created. It was later that the main bar, the Ram's Head—with windows galore—was built into one end of the mezzanine lounge.

The Blue Ox was relegated to weekend use. Our trips to Timberline fell on weekdays, and so the Blue Ox was always closed to us. We would stand outside its iron gate, peering through, tantalized. It *was* cute. It was during our 2003 vacation when Bill got the idea to ask for it to be opened for our party. When the events coordinator told us we could have it at a high rental price inclusive of a bartender, Bill countered that we didn't need a bartender. Apparently, it was then decided that we were of steady and staid age, not to mention annual guests of the lodge, and so we were granted entrance.

Wednesday evening until 10:00 or 11:00 p.m., sans bartender. $35.00.

We laid out a Tripoley game while two pre-teen boys in our group took turns playing bartender, getting a charge out of the soda spigots. We took pictures of one another against the bright glass mosaic murals of Paul Bunyan and Babe the Blue Ox. Mosaic is a misnomer. Instead of tiny squares of glass mortared all around, each colored glass chunk is cut big, the different pieces fitting together like a toddler's puzzle. The brilliant blue of Babe the ox sings against an orange ground, the bright color anchored by the black and red checkered plaid on Mr. Bunyan's lumberjack shirt. Could any other glass wall be as delightful? We were hooked.

So the next year we again rented the Blue Ox and brought a potluck of snacks and cheeses. Once again, a good time was had by all, despite having to peel down to tee-shirts because it got so warm in the little space, even with a giant industrial-strength fan roaring in the doorway. A few wandering lodge guests poked their heads in and saw a young boy behind the bar. They asked doubtfully if the bar was open, and then moved on.

Our third year holding parties in the Blue Ox, a corporate group had come along with the same idea, and though we'd already made our arrangement with management, we weren't paying the kind of fee that this other group could, and so management asked us to cut our time short. We trotted out our best appeal. Among our party was Tom and Maureen's daughter, Michaela, and her birthday was just around the corner, so we had no compunction adding that bargaining chip to the basic argument that our reservation had come first.

"You can't kick out a birthday party for a little girl!" And so they didn't. The corporate group had to do something else—or pick another night.

Our parties could get raucous. Typically, at one of the tables, a Jenga contest would be underway, soon reaching that point when one brick too many is pulled out from the teetering tower. Falling with a climactic clatter, it would regularly startle those of us who weren't in on the action, especially those "at the bar" with their backs turned. The card game at another table was just as boisterous, but it didn't matter as we were tucked into—really, a stone room—away from any other lodge activity.

The Blue Ox rental cost went up as the years piled on, and Bill passed the hat to share the expense. We could really fill that little bar. Tom and Maureen swelled their family group by hosting two of Michaela's friends, and we swelled it to even greater numbers by inviting our lodge acquaintances Larry and Maria Joao and their son Marco. Maria Joao is from Portugal and her culinary addition to our table was delicious!

And that is how some of our most indelible memories in the spacious lodge sprang from a little room originally intended for firewood.

# 13

# Losses and Gains— Timberline Goes Upscale

As the years passed, Timberline's management made small welcome improvements. Such was the early-risers' coffee and tea service. During our earliest visits, a small coffee cart had been rolled to the foot of the stairs in the ground floor lobby. This location gave sleepy-eyed denizens of the upper floors a chance to test their ski legs on the stairs, check the posted local weather forecast, pour themselves hot cups of coffee and maybe gaze at the fireplace from the rawhide-strapped chairs. A long-time assistant manager made sure empty urns were quickly replaced with full ones, and hot water available for tea, if Lipton was acceptable. We bypassed the tea, though good tea was our usual starter at home, went straight for the coffee, which was very good and stayed hot for the trip back to our rooms or to the more expansive first floor lounge. Management soon updated their tea offerings from Lipton to an array of Tazo teas. That newness of choices delighted me, as I only knew Red Rose at home. To have green tea with lemongrass seemed to fit right in on the mountain, leaving intact the sense of rustic living in a winter shelter.

From the bottom floor's limited seating, oil burner smell, and scarce daylight, morning coffee and tea service later moved to the lovely spread on the first floor set against a picture window. This was a major upgrade and a welcome luxury. Instead of rawhide-strapped chairs, the first-floor davenports spoking out from the chimney's solid rock faces became dotted with solo readers—each the first guest to wake in their party. Over the years, more and more coffee hounds began to stand and look out on the mountain, chatting softly. Rather than the camp-like experience of the cart on the ground floor, this upgrade to coffee and tea sipped in the luxury living room aimed to give everyone an expansive feel to the start of their day.

A second upgrade was that the Cascade Dining room added a fabulous buffet lunch. It's a rare feat for a buffet to be as delicious, toothsome, and healthy as it is attractive. This pulled me in even when I was dining solo, with the others out skiing, and I eagerly spread the word to them. The midday feast was on top of the fine dining in the evening, which year-in, year-out has made memorable meals from Oregon-grown delights.

Yet another gain stood out. Timberline created the nice snowshoe trail that Mary, Chris and I walked that rainy day. The genius of this simple loop trail was to keep the increasing numbers of snowshoers well apart from the skiers. To put both tortoises and hares on the ski slopes would invite disaster. Since giving up skiing, I'd taken shorter tramps up behind the lodge, where I could watch snowboarders, make a snow angel, or sit looking at Mount Jefferson and call my dad in Arizona from the mountain he knew and loved. Otherwise, the nearest place to go snowshoeing was a couple of miles east of Government Camp. Do-able, I guess, if I wanted to drive a mountain road by myself. I didn't.

As is the way of the world, not all the changes over time were as welcome to me. In time, some of the newer front desk staff had never heard of a pine marten. Increased separation of guests from the wild and non-human aspects of the lodge's surroundings subtly became the new normal, as was probably happening at resorts all over. The remote Silcox Hut, at 7,000 feet, reopened. When new in 1939, Silcox had once provided a warming shelter at the top of the Magic Mile lift. Orphaned in the 1962 relocation of the lift, Silcox hunkered in its now lonesome spot, a relic in the mists, deteriorating year by year. It took a determined group led by three climbers to save it. All this was wonderful—it was, by all accounts, beautifully renovated. The Timberline crew began driving snow-cats to Silcox with guests who wanted to enjoy gourmet dinners in an even more dramatic setting, newly accessible by ready transportation. I get that, even if the foot dragger in me preferred a Silcox shrouded in mystery, or reached only via a hard climb like our friend Larry did, seeing his breath and feeling the burn in his legs.

As things changed and the lodge got busier, the clientele seemed to include more unprepared, casual travelers and curious newbies, some with sky-high expectations. We watched as some new guests made complaints, complaints that paradoxically seemed to rise along with prices and improvements. Something wrong with their room, or the parking lot was slippery, or internet access went down, or, and this one I was on board with, lodge guests began to lose their parking places on the evenings of the expensive junkets by snow-cat to Silcox. Despite Timberline staff asking Silcox party-guests, often up from Portland only for the evening, not to park in the lot reserved for overnight guests, some took guest parking spaces anyway, and so when a carload of us were coming back from the Government Camp pub, we were aced out more than once and had to hike up from a lower parking area.

With the arrival of new and more guests, the front desk staff shifted a smidgen toward defensiveness. Though this was natural enough, I felt a ding in the we're-all-in-this-together mentality, a shared perception I had enjoyed, acknowledging we may be at a resort, but we're still in a remote and potentially harsh environment. Indeed, staff attention was sometimes needed on such things as avalanche control. As well as disabled automobiles like, ahem, ours.

Timberline's guests, on the whole, were still wonderfully nice and appreciative of the experience of being in this singular place. Nevertheless, a subtle change in the clientele didn't seem to be only my imagination. What was rare became more common, as kids and even adults began tramping (instead of carrying) their hard ski boots up and down the stairs rather than trusting the boot rack provided at the bottom, even though boots would be safe as they are in constant view of the front desk. Many of the original solid beam wooden stairs, golden, satiny, cupped and wavy from wear, are finally gone, replaced by newer pale rough-grained inserts.

In addition, I wonder if more people have so wedged their vacation into a packed modern schedule that they aren't really here when they get here. If they arrive still in go-mode, even on auto-pilot, naturally they bring their stresses with them. At least, that is how I felt, one day, when I watched a woman over-herd her children up the stairs, as if dangers surrounded them. She seemed to be making such a show of keeping her children from getting in the way that, all flapping wings, she stopped traffic altogether. Ducklings follow their parents without such ado. I wanted to tell her that children are safe here at the lodge and can be left on their own to wander and explore. I wanted these children to be allowed to notice, even if unconsciously, the unvarnished planked walls, to register this difference from the painted gypsum-board expanses of their home and school environments. I wanted to tell her that I wasn't in a hurry, nor inconvenienced by waiting for a lovely young family to pass me as I padded up the stairs in slippers with my tablet and bag of painting paraphernalia. I sought eye contact with the woman simply to give her a friendly greeting.

She caught my eye in a quick blink, followed in a nanosecond by a glance at the painting tablet under my arm. In another nanosecond she said, "Oh, that's very nice!"

I had been playing with brush lines using a new color I thought atrocious, an almost florescent orange that I was purposely wasting to get rid of it. There was really nothing to see on my paper—no recognizable image, no shading, *nothing* save garish red-orange scritches. "It is just an exercise," I mumbled, feeling patronized by what I perceived to be her reflexive, automatic praise. Then she and her ducklings were gone. My "mellow" gave way to irritation after this inconsequential encounter. I wanted my old Timberline back. I wondered, is the honeymoon over?

## 14

## The Wild West Buckaroo is Alive and Driving a Snowplow

WE WERE DRIVING BACK to the lodge from supper in Government Camp, Bill behind the wheel of our Volvo and our friends Bill C and Chris in the back seat. The road was narrowed so the highway department could do night plowing, one side at a time. We followed the red cones and crossed into a lane lined on each side by two to three feet of chunky snow stacked like a Jersey barrier. We drove on in the dimness, everything in shadowy shades of white except for the dark sky above. We were halfway through the village when something up ahead looked all wrong—we could make out something like a wall on the road. Our headlights soon lit on it. Now it was unmistakable—a huge, high pile of dirty snow accosted us, blocking the road. We were boxed in. We were going to have to back down the narrow chute.

But our situation only got wilder. The snow wall directly in front of us suddenly started to move! It got bigger and taller! We realized, despite the lack of any tell-tale beeps or visible lights, it was actually a snowplow's giant scoop, loaded to the max. We could scarcely believe what we saw next. Or, rather, what we did not see. The driver! Which meant only one thing: the driver couldn't see *us*. The scoop was inexplicably raised up in front of the plow's window, blocking what would be the driver's view. This monstrosity started toward us.

Bill threw the Volvo into reverse and laid on the horn. No response, and on it came, the hulk bearing down on us faster than we could steer backwards. I had confidence in Bill and the Volvo and didn't want to say too much, even as my anger and fear rose. We had another problem. Bill's left-side mirror was not adjusted correctly, and seeing to back up without hitting the side walls of snow was tricky. I thought to guide Bill from the right, where I sat. But Bill wanted the help that Bill C provided from the left back seat. Guys sticking together. To be fair, Bill C *is* a pilot. With his guidance, we picked up speed and put a little more distance between us and the advancing plow. Still, we urgently needed a way out. Chris and I kept scanning the ridge to our right for a low spot. When the chunked snow tapered to about 18 inches, the two Bills decided to charge it.

Now, anyone who has seen older Volvos will know that a 1999 Volvo wagon rides low to the ground. We were not cruising in one of those off-road towers on wheels seen around town. Bill put the car back into Drive and tried to blast through. The fence of snow we hit, though recently moved there by the plow, was like nearly-set cement. The Volvo high-centered, wheels spinning. We smelled something burning.

Meanwhile, the plow kept coming. We could see a sheriff's car parked about a block up ahead on the right, close to where we were aiming. Just as clearly, we could see there would be no help from the sheriff. The lawman, Bill speculated later, was probably in the late-night mini-mart making time with the female clerk. At any rate, the patrol car was empty and the plow driver was driving blind, and couldn't hear our horn. Was he rocking out with earphones and iPod?

We managed to back up, whether by virtue of the undercarriage melting the stiff snow or by some miracle, I don't know. We took another run at the barrier between us and safety, ramming it for all we were worth. Blessedly, this time, the Volvo burst through in a blinding spray to the other side, just before the plow could hit us.

Blood pressure way up and adrenaline coursing through our arteries, we were all thinking the same thing (aside from expletives): The plow driver . . . never . . . saw us.

Too stunned to stop and attempt a report, with or without curses, we made straight for whiskeys at the lodge and a return to normal heart rates. And that was pretty much all there was to the episode that Bill tagged "Double-diamond Volvo-racing in reverse."

# 15

# 2014: Disaster in a Blizzard

IF WE THOUGHT THAT a near miss with a snowplow driver in 2011 was the pinnacle of our various and sundry Mount Hood mishaps over the years, we were so wrong. The most frightening experience of my life was yet to come, one that would also sorely test my love of Timberline.

On Presidents' Day 2014, we drove the six-mile Timberline spur road up from Highway 26 to the lodge, and as we did, the weather made a whipsaw change—from warm and melty to cold and stormy.

That Monday evening, our large group of friends gathered around a picture window in the Ram's Head. We brought out our games, yet were distracted by the blizzard beating on the window. We had seen snowstorms here in other Februaries, but we all agreed this tempest was the worst we'd ever seen, the kind of winds that made clear the purpose of the rubber-tipped arm steadying the center of our large window. What's more, the forecast looked bleak—this storm would not blow itself out any time soon. Still, we were pleased to be here, and together. We turned to our card games and to catching up with those we hadn't seen in a while.

We all stayed in Tuesday and drank coffee and chatted. We played shuffleboard with the kids, who amused us with their focus on perfecting puck-slamming rockets toward their opponents. They were less interested in finessing their pucks into a scoring zone, or even in keeping the disks actually inside the table rim. Maybe let's go try ping pong, instead.

By Wednesday, though the storm continued, the wind was moderating, a little. It had gone from a howling gale to a mere gusty blow. A couple of feet of gorgeous fresh cold snow had been deposited. The warm temperature prior to the storm was forgotten, but was quietly pregnant with consequence, as the new snow rested atop the formerly melty substrate, in a layer now refrozen into hard ice.

Bill and our friends decided to try skiing the lower runs, which were the only ones with any forest shelter from the wind and thus the only ones operating. I wanted to get outside, too, and stretch my legs on the little snowshoe trail near the lodge.

I am just the average walker, and by that time in my sixties I had a good set of arthritic aches and pains. Though I knew the weather was far from ideal, I figured I could always retreat back inside if it was too bad out there. A blind assumption, I would realize. What would go wrong, and what would go right, were about to astonish me equally.

My preparations didn't take long. In our small bunk room, dim from snow that blocked the single window, I stuck toe warmers to the tops of my socks, pulled on newly purchased winter stretch pants (glad to retire my old and now-tight non-stretch shell pants), pushed into my little ankle boots, and drew my old blue rain parka over a couple of sweaters. I'd lost the lanyard for my cell phone so I slipped my flip phone into my right pocket. Bill seemed engrossed in his own ski preparations, so he surprised me when he said, "Take my GPS." He wasn't usually overprotective.

"Really, honey, I don't think I'll need that," I said.

"Take it anyway." I put the bulky tracking device into my blue jacket's ample left pocket, and squashed my thick gray hair under a brightly patterned knit hat. Ski goggles, a remnant of my old gear, I parked on my hat. Gloves and snowshoes in hand, I kissed Bill and set off down the hall. Outside, Mary was getting into her skis.

"You're going to try it today, huh, Mary?" I said, bending to cinch my boots into my scuffed Atlas snowshoes.

"Yes, no doubt it will be a short ski day," she said, smiling. "See you later." I waved and she was gone into the thick grayness.

I set my goggles carefully over my eyeglasses. I looked at my watch, pulled on my gloves and headed out. It was just after ten o'clock.

I'd walked the trail several times before, so I thought it would seem familiar despite the poor visibility. Not far along, however, I took a shortcut, hoping to get out of the direct wind, and also to cut off the first part of the trail where noise and diesel fumes infringed as snowplows worked without cease. So instead of going around the knoll on the trail, I hiked up over it through deepening snow.

As my steps sank in, I thought of the young pine marten I'd been delighted to see that morning, the first in years. He had excavated a snow tunnel right up to the glass window where a heavy carved table offered a gracious array of morning coffee and teas. Following the glass for a few feet before doubling back, he easily might have been missed, as his tunnel was further shadowed by the table's drape of white linen, but someone had spotted his weaselly face and I bent to look. What had this creature thought of his view into the lodge, fireplace alight, humans strolling around?

The knoll I was tramping, with a few stunted conifers creating pockets and shafts, would be good hunting territory for pine martens. It dawned on me that by being off the trail I was encroaching, perhaps squashing some of their unseen byways.

A gust buffeted my face. The other side of the knoll would provide no shelter—the wind was easterly, topped the knoll, and met counter-winds that eddied the falling snow. I couldn't see detail beyond a couple of yards ahead. No one else was about. Easy to see why. Only ten minutes into my walk, I decided to turn back.

Now the section of the trail I'd disdained would do nicely to get me back to the lodge. A few more steps down the east side of the knoll and I reached the firmer snowpack of the trail. I turned right and lengthened my stride, keeping track of thin red trail markers jutting up every so often through the whiteness. I wished they were closer together, but I was pretty sure I could stay on the trail. My thoughts shifted indoors—maybe I'd get out my sketch pad, fix a cup of tea.

Then without warning, I felt a funny yielding beneath my snowshoes. Not just different, *wrong*. My stomach thought faster than my mind, clenching in alarm. A second later, my left foot was standing on . . . nothing. In disbelieving horror I watched the path in front of me come apart—all slow motion and soft sounds, the surface ripping zigzag, inch by inch ahead. Like the very earth opening to swallow me. Further shocked that I could watch this instead of being overtaken by the blind chaos of a tumbling fall, I thought I must be dreaming. No, my right foot was still on the ripped edge of the trail even as the snow under my left foot slid outward from under me; like the moment a person with one foot on the dock and the other on the moving boat realizes she can no longer jump to one or the other. My arms flung out, still clutching poles. Helpless to make any other response, I sank, all but my right leg, in exquisite slow motion, remaining surreally upright.

Rising into my view was the old trail surface, my right foot still attached to it while below a crevasse-like cleft appeared. All newness creating itself in perfect pace and tandem with my descent.

The break in my world mercifully stopped widening, the creaking stilled. The rip I had watched tear open in front of me ended in undisturbed snow some eight feet ahead. I saw that the crook of my left arm rested on the left edge of a fissure in counterpoint to my right foot on the right edge. What a perch: I was inside the fissure, which was just wider than my shoulders, held by one arm and one foot. The other leg dangled straight down. Chin at the spot where my feet had stood, I marveled at the two scenes layered one atop the other: the featureless dove-gray wind-blur above and the crisp, still clarity of the steep-walled fissure below. Pure, elemental aquamarine glowed from the walls, the color leaching away where it reached the limits of light, to whiteness, then gray. I registered the privilege of seeing this sight mixed with the adrenalin of high alert.

I studied my right snowshoe. Its teeth, right under the ball of my boot, looked barely lodged. This increased my alarm at having my left leg hanging free. I looked down as best I could. There was no floor under me, only a shaft narrowing more or less regularly from my shoulders down past my dangling left leg. And on down. I wanted to see a bottom, a landing pad, white and firm. Instead, it tapered into blackness—by the rate of narrowing, I guessed another four feet lower than my foot. I tried to digest this. Why couldn't my five-and-a-half-foot frame rest in a tame little hole instead of hanging inside this nine foot drop? I was acutely aware of my isolation. No one to call out to. I was alone.

I still had my poles. With my free right arm I placed them together so that they rested across the open jaw of the fissure. This felt like a positive first action, giving me maybe a firmer hold—four more touch points—and increasing my visibility to rescuers. That hope was instantly blighted. The snow falling on my goggles told me it wouldn't be long before whiteness camouflaged me. Even so, surely the fissure itself would stay visible, if only through a shadow on its edge. I had to think so. Then again maybe not—a gusting snow flurry rushed sideways above my head, reminding me that, socked in as the sky was, defining shadows would be hard to come by. The minutes were too long and too short. I wanted to take a deep breath and break myself out. Jubilant success awaited—I only had to hurl myself left and swim, beating my way out and upwards as the teetering snow gave way. But this was not a script I was in control of. A different image leapt to mind, of snowshoes grabbed by heavy snow, knees twisted. Wait, Jean, don't be rash. You are over sixty with arthritic shoulders and bad discs, not a stuntwoman on a movie set.

How much snow was unmoored and hanging? I wished I could see behind me—how far back did the fissure go? Chagrined that my wandering mind hadn't paid attention to my immediate surroundings before the collapse, I wished mightily for a detailed memory. The only thing I remembered seeing faintly, a few steps back, was a chimney-like structure below on my left. How steep was the slope toward the chimney? Because now I was pretty sure that only the left side had moved—both sides couldn't have moved. Could they?

I needed another toehold. Trying otherwise not to move, I inched my dangling left leg to catch the snowshoe's teeth on the stronger right side wall. Sickeningly, in reaction the left side of the fissure slid further outward under my arm with a *whump* and I dropped several inches more. I *knew* it! I *knew* I couldn't squeeze down on that left arm. I let my left leg return to a dangle to recover a bit of the weight balance I'd lost. Only the end of my elbow now rested on the left edge. I looked over at this elbow with its blue sleeve now jutting out and up from my body. I didn't really need to see it to know that the arm held my weight in a way not even a healthy shoulder is built for. My right hip threatened to cramp, my hamstrings hurt—I was really doing the splits now that my right toe sat precariously perched even higher than before. I could stretch no more. I wouldn't be springing into action whatever I might wish to do. I held my body in place and tried to think clearly.

I noticed I couldn't breathe deeply, my abdominals crunching to hold my head and torso up against the backwards pressure of my high leg. A mere knee sprain now seemed like a naïve worry. To think of losing my holds and sliding farther down into icy darkness was fearsome enough, but with cold terror I knew that a different kind of fall was more likely. When the soft snow under my elbow gave way, my fall would pivot around the foot that was caught high, and I would plunge down, head first either into the narrow bottom of the fissure, or churn with the snow slab if it calved off completely. My snowshoes, which couldn't come off, would only become anchors.

It seemed that a wrong move might be my last. I'd never heard of a person buried in snow being able to tunnel out, whether in wide, awkward snowshoes or not. I pictured myself suffocating right here 400 yards from the lodge. And while part of me knew that one day I will have to say goodbye to life, viscerally I wasn't ready to die here, today. I didn't want the worst to happen to Bill, either, who bought me my first hiking boots and has walked this life with me. Nor to my mother, who climbed this mountain a decade before I was born and who now depends on me.

I would call for rescue. Yes, that's what I'd do. That I could do. A chest flutter subsided. No time to wish my cell phone were around my neck; I had to fish it out from the pocket of my jacket. My thick glove had to come off my right hand, so I reached over to my dangling left hand and used just those fingers to quietly tease off and hold the glove I might still need. Urgency and delicacy fought each other, but at least now I had something to do. I eased the phone out with my free right hand without moving any other part of my body. I pressed the emergency button on the back. I didn't know what this button was supposed to do. Maybe it was something I should have set up. I opened the clamshell and tried to see the tiny dark keys—the streaked, bulky goggles had to go. I pulled outward against the stretchy band so as to clear my glasses and lodged the goggles atop my hat. Now I could see the keypad, but only for a moment before white flakes found it. I wiped and punched 9-1-1. Nothing. My tense calm disintegrated. A second and third try. *Put it up to your ear, Jean!*

"Clackamas County 9-1-1. Where are you?" I had been down maybe four minutes, in mental overload, and I grabbed at the lifeline of this woman's voice. My words came fast.

"I'm on Mount Hood snowshoeing, near Timberline Lodge, and the snow has given way and I've fallen into a large crack."

"What county are you in?"

I blinked. What *county*? I wasn't a local. "I don't *know*. I'm at Timberline Lodge!" Fairly shouting, sure this would tell her everything.

But evidently she didn't know historic Timberline Lodge, the turn at Government Camp off Oregon Highway 26. Or maybe she heard "timber line"—tree line—and not the lodge part. "Well, the mountain is split between two counties and I need to know because they have different sheriff and search and rescue operations. Are you over by Mount Hood Meadows by any chance?"

I boggled. That was miles away, on another road. "No! I'm . . . I'm so close to Timberline Lodge, if you call them they can find me. I'm on *their* snowshoe trail."

"Is this an avalanche situation?" Her serious tone settled me a bit.

"Yes! . . . Sort of." What did I know? I didn't want to overstate this. What made me conscientious even while so frightened? Aren't avalanches those spectacular natural events featured in movies showing tons of cascading snow sending up fluffy plumes while running like a train to the bottom of a long chute? This slab had arrested itself. So far, anyway. It was no movie. I had never been to an avalanche awareness class, figuring a non-adventurer has no need for one. Even so, I'd been schooled in the last few minutes—the movement of a broad, deep, soft slab of snow is unpredictable, dangerous. "I'm below the surface," I continued. "The crack I've fallen into is unstable—it's already moved a second time. I'm worried it'll tumble."

"Hold on, I'll call them. Stay on the line. Also, do you have any health issues?"

I was warming toward her, my safety net, though I wanted her to hurry. "No, just arthritis and I'm in a bad position with one foot way up and one down." And, "My jacket is blue, and my elbow is still showing." I was thankful for every pore in its non-stick shell.

She hadn't given her name, or had she? Her inflections sounded like mine, Oregon-bred, perhaps in her thirties with a hint of fatigue—I'd bet she had kids at home.

I waited, on hold and holding on, delicately pressing the snow lip—with a slight tug toward me, as though I could keep the slab from slipping away—and just enough downward pressure to hold me up. My gloveless hand was getting cold, my hip was close to cramping. By the delay, I knew she wasn't getting through yet. Automated answering. All those mundane questions and then getting in line for a real person.

Finally, good news: "The Timberline ski patrol has been notified. They'll take their snowmobile to search from above the lodge, and the parking lot crew will come from below, so they'll find you in the middle."

I *liked* this plan. We waited, saying little, though I was glad she remained there on the line with me. Emergency responders had asked her if I had air. Something about that bothered me. I hoped they understood the rest—that the situation was unstable. I told myself not to worry, to let them do their jobs. But long minutes went by. I was tiring badly. I stared at the snow walls. So clean, devoid of life. The aquamarine color was more on the right. Did that mean ice? I saw no tunnels here, no burrows, no furry-faced pine marten for company.

Then, the 9–1–1 operator spoke again. Tension had crept into her voice. Maybe she, too, felt suspended, time ticking dangerously. "Stay on the line, I'm calling the sheriff."

My spirits sank. When she came back on the line, I pleaded that I shouldn't be hard to locate. I really wasn't far from the lodge or the day lodge parking lot. We fell silent. Then I told her I had a GPS in a pocket.

"Can you get it out?"

"I'm using my free hand to hold the cell phone, but . . ." I tucked the phone under my hat as well as I could and reached across to my left side. Of course the pocket nylon tangled, sticking to my chilled, damp fingers and wouldn't let me in. I felt the phone slip. It shot into the narrow blackness as I shouted after it, "My phone! I've lost my phone!" Hoping that she would hear and know that it was my phone and not me that had been lost. And that was the end of my 9–1–1 call. Again, I was . . . alone.

Where were my Timberline rescuers? Wouldn't I hear a team talking to each other, and calling out to me? What about the loud snowmobile? My thin sore shoulder was weakening. I was stretched to breaking. I'd felt halfway to rescue, now I was near frantic, afraid I couldn't hold on much longer. Snowflakes stuck to my knit hat, turning it white. I could wipe my glasses, but snow was getting behind the lenses, too. The search party had to be coming. Surely they understood the urgency.

"Help," I cried. I threw back my head to aim my voice upward and shouted against the sound of the wind, "Help! Help!"

And then came the most welcome words in the world. "I'm going to dig you out. Hold on." The young man's voice came from the left, down the slope from me.

For a moment I couldn't speak, discovering I'd become dizzy and slow-witted—a bad neck aggravated by the present strain. Then I managed a "Hi!"

"I saw nothing but white," he said. "And then I saw a little bit of blue."

Ah, my trusty finger-paint-blue jacket. Flat-bright, so unlike the glowing turquoise inside the snow fissure.

He dug without speaking further. I heard his shovel slice and chuck. *He is alone,* I soon realized. Not part of a well-drilled mountain rescue team, with their patter and protocol. *Will he be safe there?* He dug without grunting, which to my relief suggested he had reasonable footing. The shovel neared my arm. I didn't want the shoulder to be moved abruptly. I gathered myself again, heard my voice strangely copy this thought as though it hung in front of me like a rapidly fading cue card. "When you free it, could you not let my shoulder move abruptly?"

Through the thinning wall of snow he said as if with a smile, "That'll be me in a few years, the shoulder." Like old friends talking. I wondered if he'd had a shoulder injury, as I'd had when younger. Perhaps he was one of the avid snowboarders who were drawn to a mountain job whatever the pay. Maybe this quiet man chased thrills on the slopes. I only knew, as by a sixth sense, that he was a kind man. I felt my painful arm release from its labor, my glove still clutched in hand. Blindly, I perceived the snow becoming repacked. My left leg found a floor as he gently reworked the hanging snow inward under my snowshoe. I realized it only after he had done it. More light came through the snow on my face. The left side of the fissure now had a doorway.

Ready to help me out, he hovered, waiting to see what I needed. I pointed to my high foot. "Could you tug it down?" In a blink my foot was back in a blessedly normal position. I could test my weight on it. And now he had my hand. He pulled me out and let go of me. I hardly knew which way was up, and fell back, finding packed snow, an ersatz porch outside my former chamber. He helped me up again, I fell back again. "Maybe if I could see," I said through my vertigo.

He gently pulled off my glasses, an almost tender gesture that acknowledged my helplessness. He took off his glove, wiped the snow from my glasses. Now I got my first look at him, though only part of his pleasant face showed between his warm neck gaiter and his hat. He was in wide snow boots, not snowshoes, a yellow jacket, so not ski patrol, at least six feet tall, but not a big man. Young, yet to fill out. In my depleted state I struggled with how to ask for his name, which he hadn't said, and blurted, "What is your name?"

"James," he answered simply, at complete ease. He regarded me steadily, seeming not to mind my flat-voiced bluntness.

"Jean. Thank you, . . . James."

James helped me up again, and this time I stayed upright. Snow still swirled, but the landscape itself had stopped circling. I could smile again.

James smiled back. In his eyes I read that I was now capable of walking out. Shovel in hand, he indicated he would lead. So I followed, on my own, on wavering legs, happy for his friendly guidance down the fifty or sixty yards to his waiting vehicle. This one man had put a floor back under me, put my world back together.

He turned and helped me down from our path. At the open two-seater vehicle, I stood dumbly comparing the passenger floor well to the size of my snowshoes. I looked at James. He nodded that they should come off and indicated the cargo box on the back. So I bent to loosen the cold stiff fasteners, got free of the snowshoes, which I handed to James, and climbed into the passenger seat. He drove up the slippery road the short distance to the Wy'East day lodge, let me off at a side entrance marked First Aid, and disappeared.

My head swimming, I took in the bunkered layout, rough concrete walls. Several narrow beds formed a ward-like row, each with a red-striped grey wool blanket tightly tucked, none in use. The only person there was a trim, reserved man in a red jacket marked with the white cross of the ski patrol. He motioned me to one of the beds and I sat down on it. He stayed near the door, doing something I couldn't see, his head inclined down. No searching look from him, not like James.

The next thing I knew, Bill was there. "I'm so glad to see you!" he said, his wind-reddened face wearing a big smile, relief also swelling his chest.

I walked into his embrace. How he could be there, I didn't know, but I was *home*.

He said, "I heard by chance. I was standing at the top of the Pucci lift. Above me some ski patrol guys were talking—something about a woman snowshoer being down. I asked the name of the woman. When they answered, 'Jean'. . ." He stopped and could only exhale heavily. "Hey," he said, regaining his emotion, "you are covered in snow, Sweets, your hood is full of it." He cleaned me up, both of us chuckling, giddy. All that remained to do, it seemed, was call the sheriff, debrief to fix the trail hazard, and celebrate.

It wasn't to be that simple.

A quick account spilled out for my audience of two, Bill and the ski patrol medic. He came over to us and I stopped gesticulating to accept the tepid cocoa he put into my hand. I thanked him. I wasn't in need of warming, or refreshment, or calming. Well, yes, calming, but only after we called off the sheriff and dealt with the danger on the trail. Up through my adrenaline came a recognition: this medic did not share my alarm. The cocoa seemed there to comfort a mountain customer who had merely got herself stuck and disheveled.

I wasn't going to let him treat this like that. I explained that the sheriff might be sending responders after losing phone contact. He nodded slowly, thinking, and then punched the sheriff's number onto his cordless phone. He looked up and said nothing—another automated phone system. Odd that the first aid station wouldn't have a back line to the sheriff.

James came in, stopping just past the entry as if to avoid dripping meltwater in the warm room. His alert eyes fastened on mine where I sat, or maybe where I stood, because how could I sit quietly? With the eagerness of a first experience he said, "It was a classic avalanche situation. You were walking on an ice wall, and heavy new snow had packed against it. Your one step set it free and in motion." I beamed my thanks—he knew what I'd been in. I hoped to hear more. Bill was taking it in. I wasn't sure the ski patrol medic was as yet getting the picture.

Still waiting on the line for a live person, the medic covered the mouthpiece and directed James to go back and look for my phone. What a time for stellar customer service—he must not have understood that the snow had split nine feet down. I protested that it was just a phone. James, however, saw that the man in charge was looking at him to go. He turned and left, leaving me to regret that I didn't insist he stay inside where we could talk, where it was safe, and where I could begin to thank him in front of Bill and the ski patrol. I wanted to explain exactly what James had done, how it had been for me. Also, I wanted to know what danger remained, what he had seen that could be cordoned off so others wouldn't venture where it wasn't safe. That chance was now as lost to me as my phone, which I didn't expect could be found. James would no doubt retrace the steps that had proven safe; still, his going back alone seemed a needless risk, and this useless mission now kept us from the full debriefing that had been so close at hand.

When the sheriff had gathered my identifying information, he ended the call and I handed the cordless phone back to the medic. "Go and have a hot meal," the medic dismissed us as though to say if there wasn't an injury to splint, there was nothing more to do here. *He doesn't understand. Or maybe he is handing me off to someone else to later complete a report.* I couldn't worry about it at this moment, so flooded was I with relief. I gathered up gloves and hat, Bill took my snowshoes and poles, and we made our way through the day lodge, passing a large clock—11:30. I had been gone less than an hour and half, but the world was new, changed. We stepped outside and Bill helped me cross the icy road to the main lodge, my snowshoes left behind alongside Bill's skis.

We wanted to bask in our happiness, yet we needed to know if the trail had been closed following my rescue, to keep others safe. We stopped at the front desk. Trail closed?

She said something about the trail always being open, but she would ask. Others were listening—including Maria Joao, whose face fell as she said, "Larry just went out there!"

"Oh, we have to go after him!" I said. Just then Larry came back in, having sensibly quit his walk. I gave Maria Joao a hug of relief.

Bill and I felt the coolness of the desk clerk toward us as though to reassert that her lobby was a mellow spot in a resort that was on top of things. Which left me to feel like a mere troublemaker.

In the dining room we found our friend Mark, who looked rumpled and ruffled, and he explained that in the whiteout he'd slid off a ski run into deep ungroomed snow and had to be pulled out. My eyes widened to hear that *two* of our group had to be rescued. Mark said, "I thought I had the adventure, but you take the cake!"

In the self-serve buffet line, I found I couldn't carry my stoneware plate on my left arm, needing two hands to carry it even from one chafing dish to the next. It wasn't a matter of pain. The left shoulder had done its vital job; now it had shut down, leaving that arm next to useless. I didn't mind; *I was safe*, even if my mind wouldn't settle, waiting to bring the incident to a close and help Timberline prevent another such accident.

If the ski patrol medic didn't interview me for a report, who would? After lunch we sought out the lodge manager in her office. I introduced myself and paused expectantly, but she hadn't been looking for me and didn't even know about my accident. I filled her in, told her about where on the trail I had been, that the nearest landmark looked like a stone tower, chimney-like, below me. What would that have been? I asked. That was the water tower, she said. She was nice, and met my eyes with a smile and attention. But as I described that the trail itself had collapsed, leaving me hanging in a fissure of shocking depth, my excitement grew again as I relived my fright. I watched her lean back away from me. Though her reaction seemed sympathetic, clearly she wasn't expecting a tale like this from an agitated stranger. We knew Timberline had worked hard to keep up with the storm. This had involved early morning avalanche detail above the ski runs to release snow. But to assess the snowshoe trail by the lodge? Perhaps the possibility of a hazard *there* didn't compute, unlike the out-of-bounds terrain, which everyone understood was dangerous. She seemed uncertain what to say. She didn't ask questions or make promises to check things out. I was still in a mild state of shock even as the adrenaline was starting to wear off, and the inevitable physical pain was coming on. This was laced now with a surreal, stinging confusion as my report went nowhere. I would have fled at this point except I still needed to ask about James.

"I want to thank James, who rescued me. I don't even know his last name, only that he's on the parking lot crew."

She loosened visibly. "That would be James Myrvold," she said, and wrote the name down for me. She said she was not surprised to hear my praise, that she liked him a lot, that he had started on the housekeeping staff and was very well thought of. "Three months ago he was promoted to parking lot."

On the job just three months! I felt it would be too much to ask if I might speak with him, knowing that he and the rest of the parking lot crew continued to be beyond busy. Would she help me find out what kinds of things he likes, so I could send my thanks? She said she would be glad to.

All our skiers quit early that afternoon, and Bill C, like the good friend he is, offered me his pain medicine, which I accepted gratefully. Mary spoke in awe of such a close brush with death, and how glad she was that I was back with them. She could see I had been shaken to my core and gave me a hug that I returned tightly. In the evening, a dozen of us gathered for cards and cribbage near the mezzanine bar. They buzzed about my harrowing close call. After awhile we laughed and joked about movie rights, and how I'd want my part to be played by Emma Thompson. And Tom said that the part of James should be played by Ryan Gosling, or how about a hunk like Bradley Cooper. We settled down at the more somber thought of casting Bill's part. We couldn't have the perfect man, because Phillip Seymour Hoffman was gone.

I couldn't concentrate on cards with the group, and sat a bit aside. My euphoria papered over a whirring of emotions that I didn't know how to talk about, even with close friends. I remember Chris looking up from her game of solitaire from time to time, checking on me, and felt quiet support from others. Still, my friends, empathetic as they were, were at a resort, while I was in still in the clutch of a wilderness shock that was unknowable to others.

About ten o'clock, Bill asked if I would be able to sleep. He had stayed close by me the whole evening, laughing with me, falling silent when I did, and watching. I never loved him more. We headed downstairs to our room, walking the familiar wood-paneled hall to our bunk room.

I didn't yet know that this first night I would jerk from an exhausted drowse again and again in sensations of falling, blackness rushing at my face. Shocked afresh at how nature could so suddenly cast aside my footing, how a collapse could be so deep, and that I couldn't know how much snow was in play or what to do. Then I would remind myself I was safe. Again I would sink, also lacking a floor under me in the official reality—to my knowledge, there had been no incident report. No notes of what had happened were shared with me. She is safe, it's over. Not to me. My report of a hazard was left hanging. Most of all, why hadn't the ski patrol shown up, not reported anything? Yet there was James, who pulled me back through the broken floor and mended it for our steps out. I could only try to assure myself that the normal trail grooming routine and any guidance from James would suffice to keep others safe.

The next day the manager told me James hadn't found my cell phone. Buried just too deep. She paused, thinking about that, then said no more about it. She brightened. "James was pleased to be asked what he likes. He said that really, if you want to, just a candy bar would be nice." She smiled at this modesty, this youthful simplicity. I smiled as well—I was matching this answer to my impression of James. No, he wouldn't want to ask for anything, but he wouldn't refuse, altogether, something that came from another's heart. Yes, that's James. I only said, "Oh, I can do better than a candy bar."

Back at home, I prepared and sent a package to James, including *fancy* local chocolates. I wished I could do more. I was so grateful for James. I wanted to adopt him.

## 16

## Cousins in Survival

IN THE NEXT MONTHS, physical therapy went well, albeit slowly, and as my mental trauma subsided, I decided I would keep my snowshoes, even as I vowed to never again go out on a mountain alone. As to my thoughts of Timberline, they became tinged with a kind of . . . lonesomeness. A feeling of loss. Had my love affair of twenty years derailed? Then at tea one day at home on our back patio, I leafed through a 2010 *Audubon* magazine I had picked up from the library's free bin. A photograph jumped out, a gorgeous white weasel, its head and shoulders above the snow, looking straight at the camera. This intelligent gaze seemed to promise answers to the mystery that was so far from my city understanding: how the mountain's magnificent pine martens survived winter. Jeff Hull's article details how wilderness snow, far from a being a lifeless blanket, actually teems with life all the way down to the size of microbes; different things going on in different strata. It was a revelation to me how mice and voles, the prey of pine martens, can thrive in winter, even breeding beneath the snow blanket. These small rodents can stay warm enough at ground level, with grasses and insects to eat.

Still, I pondered what magic keeps wild creatures safe in the kind of melting, re-freezing, sliding snow that had brought me in seconds to utter helplessness? They no doubt read signs in the way snow remodels itself as it reacts to changes in temperature and reacts to weight that builds as new snow falls, or lessens as the snowpack recedes. They know their surroundings, but does that help them survive winter, especially in whip-sawed conditions?

There is no magic to their survival—Hull's article reports that wild lives are indeed precarious, and not just for an hour, the short amount of time I had hung suspended on the soft fissure edges. How it goes for little rodents, and whether they have a successful reproductive year or not, is largely how it will go for predators. His conclusion is as poignant now as when he wrote it—just as we humans finally come to discover and detail the hidden and intricately interdependent world that is alive in wilderness snow, a warming earth threatens to throttle it.

How to understand this? In referring to the seasonal timing this hidden world has enacted for thousands of years, the article was talking about it as something delicate. So a warming earth doesn't present something as simple, if I can use that word, as a unified shift—like to an earlier part of the calendar—with all of the interconnected relationships staying the same. Do I have any frame of reference for a dislocated kind of climate change? I might. A cherry orchard keeper I buy pie cherries from has recently had more than one unusual year, having to tell me she wouldn't have cherries for me. She told me the seasonal timing was off. When the trees' blossoms were open, the bees weren't yet active. Later, when the bees got going, it was too late to pollinate the cherries.

The magazine dropped into my lap as my new respect for hardier-than-me pine martens mingled with sadness for their plight. Yet, strangely, I was less lonesome about Timberline, feeling I had something in common with the mountain martens residing there. Like finding cousins, related by knowing it is all precarious. Your lives, Mr. and Mrs. Marten, as well as mine. And if life is precarious, it is the more precious, and that thought calls me to a certain seriousness in the midst of my happiness. Even long-standing Timberline Lodge, I had to acknowledge, has no guaranteed future. Special places endure with effort, and without assurances.

Now I needed to go back. What exactly had happened that treacherous day, and where, was still a puzzle to me. But James could solve it. I needed to find him again.

# 17

# 2015: My Rescuer Tells the Rest of the Story

COMING AROUND THE LAST bend, the sight that greeted us utterly confounded me. Was I dreaming? It *was* February, wasn't it? Yes, Presidents' Day, 2015. One year after the heavy snows and my accident. Why did this thin snow cover look like it was already *June*? I wasn't recognizing my Timberline. The setting had starkly altered. It was unreal.

Something clutched in me. I doubted this was simply a freak weather anomaly, like the exception that proves the so-called rule. Climate change was surely happening here.

The sad proof would come in 2023 from a photographic survey by the Oregon Glaciers Institute. Mount Hood has it even worse than some other western mountains. In 120 years, the seven major glaciers at Mount Hood have receded an average of 60%. Most ominously, roughly a quarter of that loss has come in just the last 20 years.

Climate concerns momentarily set aside, on this present snow-thin Timberline trip I had a more immediate concern to pursue. First thing Tuesday morning, I sent a message for James to the parking lot mail stop. Then I walked the snowshoe trail with Larry, who was back again this year with Maria Joao and their son Marco. On the back side of the knoll the water tower loomed up tall from the shrunken snowpack. This was what the lodge manager had thought was the chimney I'd seen. It wasn't. It was too big, and topped by a roof. Not the structure I'd passed in the snowstorm before the collapse.

Later, not having heard yet from James, I walked out again, driven by my unanswered question. I followed the now bare, dry road down the grade. I passed the day lodge on my right and came to the end of the familiar knoll rising high on my left. There I stopped in the clean, quiet air and gazed at the way the knoll fell off, the snowshoe trail wrapping around it, and then the slope continuing down. Down to what? I could now see a ways from the main road, and easy footing invited my investigation, so I turned to walk east. A few steps more and an old parking lot appeared out of nowhere. This unfamiliar lot was well below the knoll. It had always lain disguised under several feet of snow, unneeded and unplowed in winter, but perhaps in summer it served a bigger crush of visitors.

My mind was whirring. I was onto something. And soon I saw it. Along the edge of the parking lot, the side butting up to the knoll and trail, a benign sun shone on a low blocky structure banked almost all around with snow. Appearing to be built into the tapering slope, the structure was topped by something. My stone chimney. I knew it in an instant, though I had no idea what a chimney would be doing here. Buzzing with this discovery, I sobered, though with what flickering recognition I didn't know. Calmly I walked to the far end of the lot's pavement and stood for a time looking down at a precipitous ravine. My fear revisited me; had I been that close to this? How vital are trail markers! I walked back to the chimney. I thought of the dim apparition I'd seen last year, and puzzled over whether I could really have seen this from the trail.

On Thursday, the last day of our trip, James called. He'd been away for several days and had just picked up my message. He said he'd be glad to meet Bill and me after his work shift. I was excited the rest of the day—I would get to talk with James after all. Late that afternoon, down at Government Camp we three took a table at Mount Hood Brew Pub and ordered food and beer. As Bill and I got better acquainted with James and I learned particulars about him, I was not surprised to find my first impression had been spot on. It seemed I already knew the essential James. He was the same kind, smart, patient man I'd previously sensed he was when snow and fright had covered my eyes. And still so young, just twenty-four. After an enjoyable time spent learning more about him, including about his own severe shoulder injury (yes, from snowboarding), about his faith, and about how he'd recently found he had a younger half-brother who was now under his brotherly wing, I turned to what I still needed to know about my accident.

"James, today I saw a stone chimney thing down by the far parking lot," I gestured vaguely eastward. "Do you know what that is?"

"Yes. It used to be a workshop for the parking lot crew."

"Where you found me . . . I . . . I wasn't on the trail, was I?"

His face showed a dawning realization that I hadn't known, or ever been told, where I was when the snow gave way.

"No," James said.

I must have missed a tight curve westward, where the markers were too far apart for the visibility, and I'd walked southwesterly in a wider curve, on a surface packed just like the trail, above the then-buried overflow parking lot. I'd come nearer the ravine than I wanted to think about.

"Then, the ski patrol . . . ?"

"The ski patrol looked for you," James said. "Then they called us."

Oh. The news washed through me. This would explain the lack of a safety alarm about the trail surface—the ski patrol *had* gone over it. They may have come within fifty yards of me even as I clung on the phone to the 9-1-1 operator. How had I not heard them? James hadn't heard my cries, either; indeed, he'd needed visuals to find me.

Remembering that day, he said, "I saw snow above me that didn't look right, and something like a ski pole sticking up. I didn't hear you until I'd already spotted your jacket."

Nobody had had the whole picture that blinding day, and sounds were lost in the wind or to the insulation of snow; I recalled how quiet my snow chamber had been. But, thank God my untrained rescuer hadn't in his search hewed to the trail, and using his familiarity with every square yard of the area, kept his eyes honed.

Underpinnings and their limitations. Safety nets with chinks in them. Support and rescue that can come from an unexpected source. I think about these layers now—the layer I have been used to skating upon, the substrata that underlie our world, and have their own life, their own solidity, or softness. Changeable. With no promises.

# 18

# The Mural's Gift

OF ALL TIMBERLINE'S NOOKS, passages and great cathedral-high spaces, the Barlow Room has felt most like my very own special place. Now though, it's become busier, with a random staff meeting or a group from Nike or kids on the shuffleboard. I have to get up early to have that original sense of the past coming out to play. Today, however, the Barlow is all mine. I go to the window in the corner that I've been communing with for years. I'm feeling my age. Yoga is a slower and more awkward proposition than it used to be.

Once again, I study the scour-whitened mural of the sweet young woman out for a walk with her dog. I stand close to pore over details. Her hand is outstretched in a gesture to the dog, or maybe at something ahead. At her left I see only the artist's incision marks in the linoleum, no color remaining where bell-shaped flowers nod. Years after I first studied this panel I keep seeing more with each visit. On this day what I see surprises me. Above the flowers and behind the girl, a young conifer rises. I look closer at this tree. Nothing had drawn my eye there previously, but now I see a figure half hiding behind it. The figure, like the rest of the panel, is scrubbed to a soft fade, which is why I haven't noticed it before. A young man. That is . . . until I see a cloven hoof.

It's Pan! Greek god of nature and wooded glens, half man/half goat. How did I know this figure right away, especially through the barest suggestions of Lynch's depiction? Maybe, I'm thinking, we all know Pan because of the Pan flute. Or from fancifully illustrated children's books. A children's librarian tells me that myths are very popular among the young set. The colorful *I am Pan!* by Mordicai Gerstein came out as recently as 2016, calling Pan "Mt. Olympus's most lovable pest." In the adult version of the myth, Pan is shaded into a creator of noise and chaos: pandemonium, panic. There is more: he also has panache.

The artist knew the myth well, and in his murals of the seasons on the mountain, he knew to place Pan in his "Spring Walk." Lynch must have known, as I have since found, that Pan is said to have originated in Arcadia, which was a district of mountain people, culturally apart from the main Greek world. A randy beast, always after nymphs, Pan came to be connected with spring fertility.

In the mural, Pan's crisp chin is turned toward our heroine. Of course, she doesn't see.

Back to the mural as a whole. The scene's original completeness and effect can be guessed at. Now, however, eighty-seven years after its creation—the artist gone, the very lodge housing this mural having sunk perilously close to ruin, only to then be restored beginning in 1955 by prescient manager Richard L. Kohnstamm—what is before my eyes is strangely charged with fresh meaning. Cracks in the huge timbers—in the pillar at my side and in the ceiling supports—invite my imagination to travel back and then forward again. Like the lodge itself, the murals still belong seamlessly to the 1930s. More and more, though, this particular mural speaks to my own youth, when for my tenth birthday my grandmother sewed an exquisite plaid wool skirt that I loved—its pleats, stitched down from waist to hip, made charming patterns that changed as I moved, the plaid showing either light or dark with each crisp crease opening and closing. Just as the girl's skirt in the mural kicks up at her knee, it also kicks up this memory.

And it speaks to my present. Now the panel with the girl is like a dream in near white-out light. The girl's youth has faded, time has scrubbed away her fresh high color. Her dog is a ghost, a dear girlhood memory. Pan is just a whisper of a feeling, a spirit of the woods. So much is gone from the artist's original exuberance, yet this scene is as beautiful as before. Or so it seems to me.

I let my eyes sweep the entire expanse of murals, the whole story of spring, summer, fall, and winter here, the stories of generations at this place. I reflect on the memories, the seasons of my life. Over there is a corporeal image of a picnic with three generations, and I think of my Portland aunt and grandparents, camping. Further right is a joyous and comic image of a skier in the splayed, helpless posture of falling. Been there. The pack horse refusing to be led makes me recall horseback rides on experienced tricksters. Then, once again, I come back to the girl and her dog, and Pan, the one mural image that is more dreamlike, ethereal. Ruined, but also whole. Tennyson, in his epic poem, "Ulysses," describes this for me:

> Though much is taken, much abides: and though
> We are not now that strength which in old days
> Moved earth and heaven; that which we are, we are;

When the face in my mirror at home shows my lines and sags, if I recall the linoleum cut mural in the Barlow Room, I find more interest in my aging. Unlike the mural, my face was never highly colored, and now it has further paled. Still, glimmers of my history show in my smile.

I can hope that, unlike me, my old friend who still makes me smile stops aging and always retains what its carpenters, seamstresses, artists, and architects first put into it. Whatever its future, my wish is for many, many others to take enough quiet time to discover what Timberline whispers still.

# Also by this author

*The River Beyond the Dam: Shooting the Rapids of Progressive Christianity* (2023)

An ex-Christian stumbles into a progressive church—one steeped in women's equality and unafraid to free itself from outdated dogma. She still has baggage from the Christian heritage she'd rejected, and this heritage is still affecting her as an American, decades later. She embarks on a quest, like a canoe journey, with this new church community. Much like learning to paddle around fallen trees, boulders, and dangerous churn, she is helped around old thinking and mistranslation, and leaves authoritarian demands to stagnate behind their dam. What is in store for her?

# Interview

ABRIDGED FROM A 2023 Literary Titan interview:

LT: *Why was this an important book for you to write?*

I couldn't find any book like it out there. I stumbled into a progressive church almost by accident, encountering an old strand of Christianity so unlike the Christianity I knew (and had rejected) that it blew my mind. Why didn't I know about this before? The only books I could find along this line were by religious professionals—clergy, theologians—exactly the kind of book I would never have picked up after rejecting the faith.

Yet my new experience was not simply an interesting discovery I wanted to share—it was changing deep thought habits in me. I had an American habit of judging others, of turning sour when disappointed, and trying to live as a modern person who sweeps away various disappointing heritages. And these narrowing habits were being replaced by—can I say it? A happier, wider state of mind.

I thought maybe a personal memoir, with a regular person's findings of what church can be in this real world of ours, might reach and surprise general readers, especially those who, like me, had thrown out the baby with the bathwater.

INTERVIEW

*LT: What were some ideas that were important for you to share in this book?*

I wanted to encourage a deeper look at the common conclusion that we would "be better off without organized religion," even though I tended to agree with some of that, about hidebound religion. I wanted to see if I could get beneath the accrued barnacles of social control that put a few white males on top and get a look at the magnificent whale beneath those metaphorical barnacles. Just as important, I wanted to challenge the idea that, in spiritual matters, solo traveling [is] essentially the same as traveling with a community. Last, that churches can help pull together responses to the interconnected challenges of our time.

*LT: What is one thing you hope readers take away from your story?*

Whether or not you choose church for yourself, I hope that in your activism, whether on the environment or on race and gender equality, you will be open to finding allies in unexpected places.

# THE RIVER BEYOND *the* DAM
## SHOOTING THE RAPIDS OF PROGRESSIVE CHRISTIANITY

My exhilaration evaporated at the sight of the broad boulder dead ahead. I yelled to Bill, who steered from the stern of our canoe, but he didn't hear me over the frothy roar. Twisting in my seat, I jabbed my paddle in a frantic, angry arrow and re-aimed my shout backward: "Boulder!" He still didn't understand, nor see through the obscuring turmoil. Time running out, I bent to one of the few evasive maneuvers available to the bow and rehearsed the mantra we'd been taught: If you dump and are swept down river, "Keep your feet up."

When I look back on my river canoeing years, I remember our panics and our marital tussles. I remember strained shoulders and stretched elbows from hauling our first canoe, a too-heavy decked model. I remember a dump in water so frigid my chest seized and I shot straight up, a Polaris missile. The awful sound of an elephant's trumpet, but in reverse. This must have been before I got a wetsuit. But my canoeing memories also include the local paddling club we joined, friendly people with a common purpose, patient and willing to teach us.

With their class for newbies, and their coaching, we had many joyful outings on the rivers up and down Northwest Washington. One day we even were able to perch on a standing wave. We held our paddles jubilantly overhead and surfed in place. I don't know what shaped the riverbed at that spot, but whatever it was kicked up a wave that folded over on itself and stopped the forward flow there. I only know sitting atop this wave was a gas.

Despite the rougher moments, river canoeing has always rested easy on my mind—memories I'm glad to have. Even those tussles between bow and stern got laughed off over a beer.

Not sitting so easy on my mind was another part of my past, my years in Protestant Christian churches. It's not that I thought of those days often. But it's funny how the past doesn't always resolve neatly into one's life story but can stay tucked on a back shelf, like canned goods long past their pull date and maybe even bulging ominously. My strains and pains in the churches of my youth and the memory of Christian strictures on women still nettled me occasionally, even decades after I left. A mere glimpse of devotional books in a store window could make me flinch. I would think about how, for the devout, the honeyed devotionals held in place the status quo—"Trust and obey, for there's no other way..."

Unlike the friendly group of experienced paddlers who accepted me fully, the adult Christians I remembered while a sophomore in high school in the Panama Canal Zone seemed to be not with me, really, but only acting a role. A handful of the Panama Christian youth group became good friends, regular kids who could be teased for ordering gravy on their French fries (in the muggy hot tropics, no less) at the Balboa military base hangout, and who got weak in the knees like I did for such pop songs as "Unchained Melody." Having a community of friends there is a sweet memory. But as far as Wednesday night prayer meetings and soulful witness and Sunday services and Christian counseling went, I didn't want to remember my church years at all and was sure I'd never go back.

www.ingramcontent.com/pod-product-compliance
Lightning Source LLC
Chambersburg PA
CBHW071716040426
42446CB00011B/2090